THEORIZING TRANSGENDER IDENTITY
FOR CLINICAL PRACTICE

THEORIZING TRANSGENDER IDENTITY FOR CLINICAL PRACTICE

A NEW MODEL FOR UNDERSTANDING GENDER

S.J. LANGER

Jessica Kingsley *Publishers*
London and Philadelphia

First published in 2019
by Jessica Kingsley Publishers
73 Collier Street
London N1 9BE, UK
and
400 Market Street, Suite 400
Philadelphia, PA 19106, USA

www.jkp.com

Library of Congress Cataloging in Publication Data
Names: Langer, S. J., author.
Title: Theorizing transgender identity for clinical practice : a new model
  for understanding gender / S.J. Langer.
Description: London ; Philadelphia : Jessica Kingsley Publishers, 2018. |
  Includes bibliographical references.
Identifiers: LCCN 2018005668 | ISBN 9781785927652
Subjects: | MESH: Transsexualism--psychology
| Gender Identity | Transgender
  Persons--psychology | Psychological Theory
Classification: LCC RC451.4.G39 | NLM WM 611 | DDC 616.890081-
-dc23 LC record available at https://lccn.loc.gov/2018005668

British Library Cataloguing in Publication Data
A CIP catalogue record for this book is available from the British Library

ISBN 978 1 78592 765 2
eISBN 978 1 78450 642 1

Printed and bound in Great Britain

Contents

Acknowledgments

In the solitude of writing the book there were many people on whom I relied and I was humbled by their support. I am indebted to my co-presenters and audiences at various conferences where I presented many of the ideas offered here. These include the Philadelphia Trans Health Conferences, World Professional Association for Transgender Health Symposiums, U.S. Professional Association for Transgender Health Symposium, White Institute, National LGBT Health Conference, Working Group on Gender at New York State Psychiatric Institute's Division of Gender, Sexuality and Health and The Science of Consciousness Conference. Especially, ICP's Psychotherapy Center for Gender and Sexuality's Trans Clinical Biannual Symposiums in New York City and particularly the co-directors Joanne Spina and Bob Najjar who have been very supportive of me and my ideas. I received invaluable feedback from the discussions which ensued in the Q&As, as well as on walks and water taxis, during meals and Skype calls, and over countless coffees around the world. Christopher Bussman and the staff at the School of Visual Arts Library were instrumental in acquiring the literature and research for this book and were undaunted by my constant flurry of interlibrary loan requests. Thank you to my lawyer Jonathan Lyon for his invaluable advice. Gratitude to Adriana Passini for shaping my clinical thinking over these many years. Thanks to Laura Erickson-Shroth, Kathleen Delmar Miller, Judy Luhr and Robert-Paul Juster for their solid and helpful feedback; and to my chair, Debi Farber, at the School of Visual Arts' Art Therapy Department and all my colleagues, especially Val Sereno and Liz DelliCarpini for their support and encouragement and adopting me into the department. For their intelligent comments, detailed suggestions, support and treasured friendship: Christie Block, Luc-Olivier Charlap, L. Zachary DuBois, Judith Jordan, Julie Lipson, Jae Puckett, Jack Pula and Karalyn Violeta. My gratitude and thanks to my supportive friends Tina Andreadis, Sam Eber and Peter Walsh. Thank you to my CM family for all the unconditional love during this process. Thanks to my supervision group, Kathy Panos, Daisy Alter and Ellen DiMeglio, for over a decade of conversations, support and comments on various chapters. To my patients who honor me with the trust of being their therapist, I thank them for allowing me into their lives. I hope they feel my dedication to them and that I have done them justice in this work. I could not have endured the hours at the computer without the help of Nina Simone. Thank you to Debra Rosenzweig, for being my compassionate mirror and container. Deep appreciation to Chris Straayer for his friendship, mentorship and tennis. Thanks to everyone at JKP including Emily Badger, Hannah Snetsinger and my editor, Andrew James, whose calmness, responsiveness and invaluable advice has made this a smooth birthing process. With all my deepest love, gratitude and dedication I thank my wife, Denise, for always believing in me and for being my family.

Introduction

I arrived at the writing of this book as a psychotherapist in private practice in New York City, initiated into the field as a new graduate in the spring before September 11, 2001. My graduate independent study project was an article critiquing the validity of the gender identity disorder in childhood diagnosis in the psychiatric nomenclature (Langer & Martin, 2004). These two quite separate events organized my thinking and professional trajectory as a gender specialist and a trauma specialist.

This book is the cumulation of years of creating treatments with my patients, presenting at conferences, debating over breakfasts, listening on walks, processing in supervision groups and disagreeing in professional meetings. l am offering a new model of how to think about and comprehend gender, which extends our understanding into the inside of our bodies. The clinical recommendations are rooted in clinical trial and error, specifically focusing on select clinical subjects in relation to trans experience which need more therapeutic discourse, such as trauma, sex and disability (since to focus on all clinical issues would be encyclopedic).

When l was in film school, we were constantly told to make the film you would want to see, so I have carried this edict with me through writing this book. It is the book I wish had been there for me and which I hope will fill a void for others, professionally and personally. This book is not an introduction to trans experience; there are other competent books for that purpose. My book is a next step, a deeper step into the complexity of gender.

The book ventures to provide an existential phenomenology and ontology of trans identity and expression. I will introduce a conceptualization of gender as a core aspect of consciousness which can be understood through the free energy principle in order to explain the feeling of gender disequilibrium. My project is not a simple one but, despite my trepidation at an inability to say everything at once, I will further the understanding of gender in general, and trans/gender diversity specifically. The reader should be cautioned that I do not propose that I can possibly speak for every trans person's experience as this is not a monolithic community. Specifically, within this book, I will be talking about my experiences working with people (from a cross-section of New Yorkers who could find their way to a private therapist, which I acknowledge is a biased sample), some of whom sought me out in order to explore gender and others who began treatment for other clinical reasons and gender came into the picture secondarily. At the moment, fifty percent of my full-time private practice is with people who identify as trans or gender diverse. Additionally, I am including examples from novels, art, memoirs and other accounts by trans people to diversify the lived experiences illustrated.

There are fundamental differences between trans/ gender studies and how mental and physical health clinicians approach individuals if/when they do become patients. This was particularly clear to me when in 2016, within a few months of each other, I participated in the World Professional Association for Transgender Health Symposium in Amsterdam and the first International Trans Studies Conference in Tucson. There were only a handful of the same people at both conferences, even though each group (and certainly discussions in presentations) would have been enriched by attending both. Health professionals would have a better approach towards patients with more critical theory from the humanities, and academics should not feel shut out of learning from and contributing to the medical/mental health process for transgender people.

I will work to bridge these two fields, which are significantly siloed from each other. The deeper and finer we seek to understand anything, the more complex and interdisciplinary we must become. This is especially true for transgender lives since medical, psychological, philosophical and other disciplines are needed practically and theoretically to achieve recognition and equilibrium in one's gender.

Although this is a clinical and theoretical book, it is not to imply that trans identity, experience or expression is a pathological condition. It is not. It is a variation of gendered existence in humans. The recognition that the tide runs this way is gaining strength and the more gender is unmoored from psychiatric nomenclature the less pressure there is for gender to conform to certain diagnostic structures (Robles *et al.*, 2016). The major goal of the book will be to inform clinical practice with people who happen to be trans and gender diverse. Professionals from all the mental health fields (psychiatry, psychology, psychoanalysis, social work and creative arts therapy) who are not knowledgeable about gender will be able to use what they know from their fields to understand my formulation of gender and how to apply it to clinical practice.

It is also my aim to further the understanding of gender in a general sense. Even though the following is written in the language of clinicians and academics, it is no less intended for the non-professional person. It is for the person who is alone, working out how to understand the feelings happening inside them and that their feelings may have no other explanation but this elusive bundle of sensations we call gender.

The early chapters could be dense depending on the reader's background and sense of adventure in learning from new fields, but my hope is that it will be worth the effort. I know it might be frustrating, but gender is complicated, and a new complex theory is necessary before we approach clinical work. It is a wide net I have cast but I believe we cannot know gender at its more microscopic levels without expanding outside of the fields of psychology and psychoanalysis. Neither of these fields yet effectively understands gender without pathologizing some forms of it. The early theoretical chapters will provide the foundation and frame from which the clinical work discussed later is assembled. The theories from other disciplines have been exciting to learn about but may seem like unusual paths for a therapist to follow. I was initially captivated by the research on interoception and consciousness, which led me deeper to the free energy principle. All of these concepts come from the overlapping disciplines of neuroscience, neuro-psychoanalysis, consciousness studies, biology, philosophy and physics. If we want to understand and drill down to the core of any phenomenon, it is impossible not to utilize interdisciplinary tools.

Chapter 1, Being and Knowing, will begin with an explanation of how we know what we feel and how we connect to our internal sensations by drawing on the psychophysiology and neuroscience of interoception. I am amplifying the internal experience of gender in this theory to demonstrate that the core of gender is more than just body-image and the visual realm. I will construct a theory of gender based on the free energy principle which is a unifying theory of neuronal processes that was developed in the beginning of this century. By using this new theory, I will develop my own new theory of how and why we feel gender. The concept of gender dysphoria will be relocated as a type of "free energy" as opposed to mental illness. This is a distinctly different orientation towards neuropsychology and gender. The field has mostly been focused on sex-dimorphic areas of the brain, which is just as narrow as locating gender only in sex-dimorphic genitals. My approach does not discount any part of the body or mind and substantiates that gender is an interactional process across mental and physical systems of the human organism.

Focusing in on the nature of gender, in Chapter 2 I will explain my theory of the foundational nature of gender in consciousness. Damasio, Craig and others in neuroscience and consciousness studies will be relied upon to connect gender within the development of the self, as part of consciousness. I will examine why gender identity remains stable, even in the cases of brain injury. Gender identity remains stable as long as we have consciousness. Therefore, gender is core and inseparable from consciousness, which leads me to theorize gender as a foundational segment of our basic humanity. As such, the following chapters propose a way of understanding and working with gender based on its intrinsic importance in our beings.

The development of the self through the psychoanalytic and developmental psychology theories of mirroring will be explored in Chapter 3, Mirroring Recognition, within the context of when that mirroring runs contrary to the felt gendered self of the child. This chapter is an expansion and revision of ideas which began with my article "Trans Bodies and the Failure of Mirrors" (Langer, 2016). The implications of this on the development of attachment, shame and internalized transphobia will form an interactional developmental model of the experience of being a child who is trans or gender nonconforming (TGNC). When I say TGNC child, I include those who know or who do not know yet that they will identify in that manner. This includes kids who know they are trans, kids who are seen as gender nonconforming, and trans adults who retrospectively give an account of their childhoods before they understood they were trans.

Chapter 4, Gender, Terminable and Interminable, is an exploration of the continuous discovery of gender through my algorithm of gender. This is a formulation that balances the various elements of the gendered body and behavior which make up gender expression, while considering the level of importance these elements have for the individual. These elements create the equation which adds up to the person's gender identity. The equation calculates across and between gendered elements to equate to a gender equilibrium. This formulation is a clinical stance and tool to work with gender in treatment.

Chapter 5, Accommodating for Bodies, will provide a clinical discussion on sex through the lenses of disability studies and sex therapy, along with physical and mental health. How do we understand the possible impairment in sexual functioning physically and psychologically for trans bodies? The implications of eugenics, disability, prosthetics and shame for trans bodies and psyches will be interrogated and practical clinical techniques will be offered based on the preceding theory.

The final chapter, Trauma, Trans and Temporality, is in two parts. The first is the trauma of trans time. Trans time captures the unique relationship to time for trans people. It will cover the consequences of the developmental slippage which can occur during transition, the lost time never to be recovered and the lost time during medical leaves. In the second part of the chapter, I will turn attention to the clinical nuances of understanding and working with gender trauma, particularly in conjunction with other acute and chronic traumas treated in psychotherapy.

My overarching points are to highlight the internal feeling of gender when it is in and out of regulation, how non-binary it is and that gendered feelings lead rather than follow identity. I heard in a yoga class the other day that "it is not the form that matters but the sensations in your body." This is the grounding principle of my theory: listen to the body. My aim is to show the developmental and interpersonal strain experienced by trans people through shame and trauma. All of this is to ensure a superior psychotherapy for trans people who do need or want treatment.

As the book progresses there will be more focus on clinical practice. The clinical material is drawn from my practice with the permission of some of my generous patients. It does not include everyone from my practice since it would not have been appropriate to their treatment to ask some people for permission. To all my other patients who are not mentioned but who were still intrinsic in influencing my thinking on this subject, I am also grateful. I have specifically only included short clinical examples and not extensive clinical material from any one person out of respect for their privacy. It is exceedingly difficult to be detailed without revealing too much of a person's identity. Additionally, I do not feel that their whole stories are mine to tell and do not want to contribute to a history of objectification of trans experience. To supplement, I will also draw from the memoirs and art of trans artists whose work is relevant to this project. The point is to highlight certain moments in clinical work with trans people rather than to illustrate an entire treatment process or every clinical incident. This is not a survey but a specific examination of new theories and select clinical moments which require further inquiry.

It is more critical than ever to be theorizing gender from a non-pathological frame. There is still a split in transgender health as evidenced by who is recognized as an expert in the field (i.e. can say they are a gender specialist, chosen to speak at conferences, featured in documentaries, etc.) and who and what is included in how research and practice are deemed appropriate and ethical (i.e. what constitutes conversion therapy, is preventing a trans outcome a valid goal, who is on diagnostic nomenclature committees, standards of care working groups and other powerful committees, etc.). If we are to advance the field in the direction of empowering individual positive recognition of gender which includes access to interventions without obstructionist protocols, then we must have theories and practice that do not only rely on disease models and binary formulations of gender. Only then will we improve the lives of trans people and free everyone from gender rigidity.

This book is a work of passion: for clinical work, for gender theory, for trans health and community. The beginning of the book is the most vigorous part of our journey together, but much like hiking, it's steep in the beginning but that's part of the adventure. As much as there is to absorb, it will be reinforced through the clinical discussions coming afterwards. I hope the ideas will push the reader to think differently about gender, our psyche-soma and our clinical approach.

CHAPTER 1

Being and Knowing

The Interoception of Gender

We cannot just think our way through understanding gender. It is not an objective process. We are well advised to heed neuroscientist Bud Craig's words, "I feel therefore I am" (2015, p.xvii). To understand the body we must engage not only our mind; we have to be attuned to our body as well. "The nature/nurture debate is meaningless in the context of human mental functions..." (Ramachandran, 2004, p.108). Ramachandran equates it to asking if it is the hydrogen or the oxygen that makes water wet. The study of the nature of gender in mind and body is no less separable than deciphering if the wetness of water comes from the hydrogen or oxygen. Gallese (2014) warns us that we cannot look for the self in the brain on its own but must look at the interconnections between brain processes and the body. By the same token, this is what has been proposed with our approach to gender in recent years; we cannot rely on the appearance of one's body to predict a person's gender. This is why I am foregrounding the interoceptive nature of gender here.

In line with that thinking, I will take understanding gender a step further to state that we cannot discount the communication between the mind and body on the subject of gender. The following will be the foundation of my internalist theory of gender. This is a phenomenological perspective which explores the internal, private, embodied gendered experience of the individual. My goal in this chapter is to apply interdisciplinary theory to further the understanding of how one feels, perceives, understands and identifies their gender. First, I will establish gender as a psycho-physiological process through exploring the phenomena of interoception and exteroception. I will then build on the process of understanding gender by explaining it through the free energy principle, which is a theory from computation neuroscience that describes embodied brain processes. I will illustrate what and how it feels like to be transgender. This chapter will work as a base for the rest of the book, so that we are working from the same orientation. This way we can look at how gender functions in or complicates people's lives and how therapists can work with their patients through these knotty forests.

The signifier trans will be used as shorthand to describe the myriad of people who either question their gender, make changes to their body and/or behavior in a gendered manner or who identify across the gender spectrum. When speaking about specific people, I will use their preferred identifier and pronoun. It should be noted that I am *not* taking a binary view here of gender (and will explain why) or a binary view of most other phenomena: mind/body, reason/emotion, male/female, etc. Additionally, I aim to debunk the myths held by society and internalized by trans people that one's gender identity is chosen, is not "real" or is a means of deception (Rood *et al.*, 2017).

This chapter will plumb the subtle and nuanced perceptions of the body in conscious and non-conscious awareness and processing. It will also make the argument for the elements of gender that are not in the visual field and develop a theory by which to structure these landscapes. To more fully develop our understanding of trans bodies for trans selves, clinicians and theorists must de-emphasize the visual realm of the body and move inside.

I will be working with certain terminology from physiology and will orient the reader to those terms. I have gravitated towards this orientation to coordinate the psychophysical nature of gender within my theory to include how we sense and perceive our bodies internally and in time and space. I am dislocating trans away from a biomedical model in which symptoms are proven to an objective observer and reorienting it to a psychophysics perspective that is tangibly situated in the individual's subjective experience in which the individual is the expert. This perspective will still include theories from psychology and psychoanalysis but will additionally incorporate neuroscience and philosophy of perception. I am following the definitional difference that privileges the phenomenal experience of the person over what kind of neural receptors define interoception, proprioception and exteroception. This simplifies things and keeps us focused on the experience of the individual.

So, I will work from the outside in and start with exteroception. This is the perception of stimuli originating from the outside of the body. It includes what we see and hear and also temperature and sensation on our skin. It is what we take in from our environment. In relation to gender, it is how we see, hear and feel from outside ourselves.

Proprioception is the channel and interpretation of various sensory input from the musculoskeletal system and the skin connected to movement, orientation in space, and kinesthetic information coming from the muscles, tendons and joints. Proprioception falls under exteroceptive senses (the perception of the outside world);

even though it is a feeling in the body, it is about the body in space. The perception of motor activity provides the individual with multisensory information about the body and its interaction with the environment (Gallese, 2014). This is the perception that keeps us from bumping into walls and allows us to walk without watching our legs and consciously commanding them to move.

Finally, and key to understanding gender, is interoception. It is the physiological sense of the internal body and the engine of our subjective feelings (Craig, 2009a; James, 1890/1950). Interoception is the perception of our internal viscera (also known as visceroception). Historically, visceroception and interoception have at times been used to describe some of the same phenomena but it is generally accepted now that interoception is the defining overarching term. Interoceptive awareness is the sensing of the internal milieu of the body, from receptors in the cardiovascular, gastrointestinal, respiratory and urogenital systems (Ádám, 1998). It also encompasses nociceptive (pain) stimuli, somatic stimuli and all other internal senses of the state of one's body and regulating homeostasis. Interoception is a key aspect to the process known as the salience network (Uddin, 2014). The salience network is a function of our brain which highlights which stimuli are important to act on and determines what homeostatic or allostatic regulatory functions will be carried out to maintain the body. These drive behavior in order to ensure regulation and integration which includes behavioral function, and the endocrine and neural systems (Craig, 2015). Homeostasis is when our non-conscious internal systems automatically regulate the internal milieu when an error has occurred, e.g. our glucose levels are too high or too low (Sterling & Eyer, 1988). Allostasis is when our brain "uses prior knowledge, both innate and learned, to prevent errors and minimize them" and communicates with the body to return the organism back to stability (Sterling, 2014). The allostatic process is volitional and anticipates and adapts to the environment.

Interoceptive processes can be conscious and non-conscious, but they primarily involve conscious awareness until there is a problem, like hunger or shortness of breath. The perception of one's own gender is an interplay of all these processes, not only the visible characteristics of gender. What follows will detail how this occurs and why it is important for the well-being of trans people.

Core gender

My preliminary proposal relates to a pre-definitional aspect of gender identity I am calling core gender. Core gender is a psychophysiological phenomenon which is the result of interoceptive and exteroceptive (but not interpersonal) information. This is similar to the private (internal sensations) and public (observable bodily aspects) body consciousness that Miller, Murphy and Buss coined (1981). Gender is a psychophysical phenomenon made of material bodies, emotional minds and interpersonal processes (Chapter 3 will address the interpersonal). Core gender is a hidden cognitive process, one among the many that occur within every human being. It strives towards its own unique stability, which is an underlying building block of gender identity.

Interoceptive, proprioceptive and exteroceptive information affects the brain and body to ensure gender equilibrium. Homeostatic sentience is a "real-time" interoceptive picture of one's being; the feeling of living in one's body (Craig, 2015). Gender is a part of our sentience since the feeling of one's self in a body is particularly gendered (along a spectrum of gender). If aspects of gender identity and expression are not aligned for the individual, their equilibrium is dysregulated. The byproduct of this dysregulation is what psychiatry calls gender dysphoria. In cisgender people, their gender identity and body are in equilibrium and they do not experience an incongruence between psychic gender and material body and therefore do not feel gender dysphoric. For trans people, their gender initiates the feeling of error within their body, a kind of enhanced interoceptive surprise. The human system can try to regulate or adapt but will not find homeostasis (this will be discussed further later in the chapter).

The elements and regulatory participants of gender (which can be disturbed in dysregulation) include proprioceptive (musculoskeletal), interoceptive (internal organs/systems including the brain) and exteroceptive (visual and skin) afferent (body up) and efferent (brain down) signals (see Figure 1.1). These function in what is called a resonant loop and are part of the salience network communication. Interoception is afferent and the visceromotor response is efferent signaling (Uddin, 2014). There are gendered aspects to many of these systems which are individual in nature; no one's gender is exactly the same as anyone else's since their afferent and efferent information/response is unique.

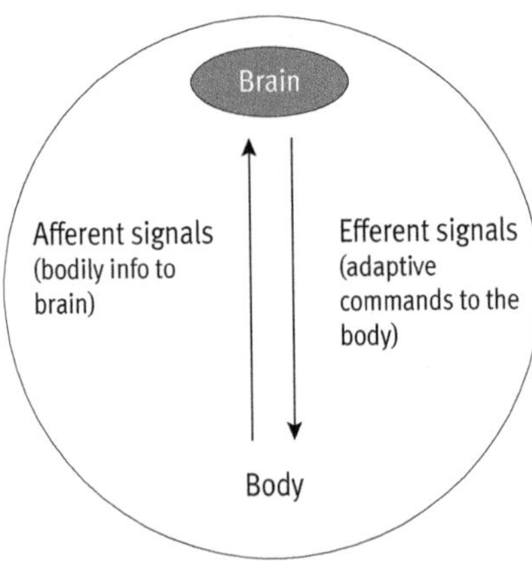

Figure 1.1 Body and brain signalling

How our sensorimotor structures are configured in the brain is that the insular cortex registers the feelings while the cingulate cortex provides the motivation to act on it (Strigo & Craig, 2016).[1] Feelings from the body and the motivations towards acting on them are what Craig calls homeostatic emotions (2009a). This is the pathway on which I am building the case of gender dysphoria as an emotion based on dysregulation, as a feeling of a kind of psychic allostatic load,[2] psychological wear and tear on the individual. One trans woman described it this way: "It is like you've been wearing a really itchy suit your entire life and didn't know, until now, you could take it off" (Henry, 2017, p.25).

According to the physiologist György Ádám (1998), the defining feature of unconscious behavior is that is consists of interoceptive percepts influenced by humoral-hormonal and proprioceptive information. Information that arrives in the brain has four different transformational aspects: physicochemical, physiological, psychological and behavioral (Ádám, 1998). There are gendered elements to each of these aspects: hormonal, genital shapes, understandings of our gender, the feeling of gender, gendered gestures and other expressions, to name a few. Suffice it to say, most of these processes are non-conscious. Most of our mind is non-conscious, we only know of its existence from the surface of consciousness (Damasio, 2010). There is developing consensus that interoception is a substantial aspect of our sense of body ownership which is a multi-layered process that includes attention, detection, sensitivity, accuracy, etc. (Seth & Friston, 2016).

---

1   The insular cortex is the hidden lobe of the brain in the Sylvian fissure which functions to give emotional context to physiological experience. The cingulate cortex is part of the limbic lobe and is implicated in emotion processing as well as memory and learning.
2   Allostatic load is defined as the physical wear and tear on the body of chronic stress.

Later we will look clinically at how this process plays out in relation to gender.

Dichotomous theory of the body versus body matrix

More nuanced definitions for understanding bodies are needed. Recently I applied the philosopher Shawn Gallagher's concepts of body-image and body-schema to the understanding of gender (Langer, 2016). The following will summarize this dichotomous theory of the body. Then I will move on to how a body matrix approach is more useful in gender theory.

Body-image relates to the appearance of the body in the visual field and the accompanying beliefs and attitudes, which include the individual's perceptual and conceptual understanding and emotional experience of the body (Gallagher, 2005; Gallagher & Meltzoff, 1996). It perpetually and actively affects our perceptions and facilitates the feeling of ownership over the body and sense of self (Gallagher, 2005). It is not innate but develops in infancy between six and 18 months, during the time of the mirror stage (Gallagher, 2005; Lacan, 1966). Concurrently during this time in development, exteroception (perception of stimuli from outside the body) begins to supersede interoception (perception of sensations from the internal milieu of the body including autonomic, hormonal, visceral and immunological signals) which was privileged in utero and during infancy (Ádám, 1998; Craig, 2003). Chapter 3 will expound further on the mirror stage and its relation to child development in trans children and adults. Here I will focus on body-schema and its importance to understanding core gender.

While body-image comes out of the visual field, body-schema receives its signals from internal milieu. Gallagher (2005) defines his body-schema as consisting of proprioceptive awareness and information alone. Body-schema functions to integrate the body and environment for the individual. It was essential in my formulation to include interoception because one's internal sense of being is foundational for gender.

However, with the inclusion of interoception and understanding gender dysphoria as an allostatic emotion, the theory of a body matrix seems more applicable. Body matrix is a theory of the body as a multisensory (interoceptive, exteroceptive, proprioceptive) neural representation of the body which serves to integrate and modulate physical and psychological equilibrium of the organism, which also includes adapting to external circumstances (Moseley, Gallace & Spence, 2011). The body matrix is constructed from multisensory input which then develops into somatotopic representation[3] of the body. Then there is body-centered spatial representation (the orientation of our body in space) and peripersonal spatial representation (the immediate space around our body) that become integrated into our body map. This body matrix runs in contrast to the dichotomous body-image/body-schema because it proposes that the body matrix is about maintenance of homeostasis of all these functions (Moseley, Gallace & Spence, 2011). The body matrix is then implicated not only in stability, physically and psychologically, but also in the systems that effect change in those elements to bring them into alignment. This formulation captures the multilayered and interconnected nature of systems across the body/brain/mind which relates more to the complexity of gendered experience.

Damasio (2010) expands on how the brain and body communicate. The body communicates how it is

---

3   Somatotopic representation is the organization and coordination within the brain of somatosensory information coming from various areas of the body within the motor regions of the brain.

made and how it should be seen to the brain. The brain signals back how to maintain that regulation through homeostasis and allostasis and provokes the body to create an emotional state through neural and chemical (including hormonal) channels which can be initiated from thoughts. Many of our emotional states are the mind's interpretation of the state of the body. If we look at the brain areas involved, the relationship may seem clearer. One of the functions of the inferior parietal lobe is interpreting sensory information along with the anterior insula. In addition to body representation, the anterior insula is implicated in subjective emotion processing. The limbic structures are also known as the emotional motor system. The interactions of these regions work to represent the body-schema. The insula is the neural correlate of interoception (Craig, 2009a; Damasio, 1999). Moseley and colleagues (2011) propose seven brain regions involved in the body matrix: premotor, operculum, superior parietal, primary somatosensory cortex (S1), posterior parietal, insula and the brainstem. There have also been discoveries of other regions called the extrastriate body area (EBA) and the fusiform body area (FBA), which respond to recognizing bodies but not faces (faces activate the fusiform face area (FFA)) (Berlucchi & Aglioti, 2010). Moseley and colleagues (2011) believe, given these structures and thinking through an evolutionary model, it makes sense that a rough proto-representation of the body exists that can accommodate different shapes within minimal constraints.

This specificity about the brain is just to note the many areas involved in our maintenance of the state of our body. Furthermore, the state of one's body necessarily includes gender, which is necessarily inclusive of multiple aspects of feelings from within the body. I will demonstrate how there are a myriad of ways we feel gender, not just from our primary and secondary sex characteristics but from our other viscera as well.

Hormones

When thinking about the neurological, cardiovascular, gastrointestinal, respiratory, and urogenital systems in relation to hormone treatment, the genital region may seem at first like the most sensitive to hormone changes, but it is not the only system implicated. Musculature changes, shifts in fat distribution (an increase in visceral fat), emotional reactivity and metabolic changes can all make a dramatic shift in response to hormones (Auer *et al.*, 2016; Elbers *et al.*, 1997; World Professional Association for Transgender Health (WPATH), 2011). The metabolic changes include a decrease in alanine, lysine and citrulline levels in trans women and an increase in trans men (Auer *et al.*, 2016). The other shifts listed have gendered interoceptive and exteroceptive associations attached to them (e.g. fat distribution can appear feminine or masculine). The metabolic changes appear to be gendered and probably have a distinct interoceptive feeling but are less easily articulated. Is this why trans men describe an increase in appetite? According to Ádám (1998), for much of the visceral system, it is impossible to give a precise border where interoception ends and exteroception begins (e.g. the urethra is an interoceptive region but the penis also has exteroceptive qualities). These are usually out of conscious awareness.

The interoceptive systems have chemoreceptors which detect and are affected by hormone levels among other changes in the blood; the hypothalamic and bulbar structures are particularly sensitive to hormone levels (Ádám, 1998). The hypothalamus monitors and regulates the internal viscera, including hormone levels, and is a central player in the integration of somatosensory and viscerosensory information (Ádám, 1998; Damasio, 1999). Visceroception/interoception includes the internal milieu which is transmitted through the bath of chemical molecules in the bloodstream which communicate both to and from the brain (Damasio, 2010). We need a preliminary understanding of these systems to have a sense of the multitude of signals the individual is processing at every moment, including gendered sensations. The lining of some internal organs of a trans man with exogenous testosterone undergoes a thickening, similar to what happens to the skin, whereas other organs atrophy such as the ovaries and vaginal walls (WPATH, 2011). What effect is that having on the body matrix? What is the gendered sensation of the intestinal tract? Is that the culprit in increased appetite? Is it even the intestinal tract or the brain? When a trans woman's skin softens, is that happening to her internal organs as well? What are the interoceptive percepts of her viscera? What about those internal sensations which were gender incongruent before hormone treatment that were impossible to articulate but now feel succinct? I am laying the groundwork for refocusing gender back inside the body and relying less on exteroceptive processes to feel and know gender. It is already fairly complicated for someone to know how they feel in their gender by comparing how their body looks with how it feels; but it is an even more herculean task to compare how they feel in their body with how it might feel with exogenous hormones. The right anterior insular cortex (AIC) is implicated in male sexual lust, anxiety and depression (Craig, 2015). So does increased blood flow to genitals alone result in higher sex drive with testosterone in trans men? Or is it something happening in the brain? Most likely the process includes multiple sources.

What is the variability to feeling one's interoceptive gender?

There is variety in interoceptive accuracy (lAcc; how accurately one can consciously feel signals from the internal milieu) across the population. This is considered the objective dimension of interoceptive ability, the subjective dimension being called interoceptive sensibility. The interaction between these two is called interoceptive awareness (Craig, 2015; Garfinkel *et al.*, 2015). lAcc is how we listen to our internal sense of our bodies by a process in three stages: afferent signaling (body to brain signals), paying attention and then evaluating the perception (Schulz & Vögele, 2015). One way it can be determined is by a correlation between an individual's ability to accurately perceive their heartbeat. Subjects lie in a quiet room subjectively counting their heartbeats while a machine objectively measures their pulse and a comparison is made between the two counts. The more accurate the count is, the higher the person's lAcc. It has been hypothesized within a general population that those with higher lAcc have a more positive body-image operationalized as body satisfaction, body identification, perceived self-control of the body, and lower hypochondria and sexual dissatisfaction (Duschek *et al.*, 2015). Additionally, those with higher lAcc are better able to feel their emotions, know their emotions and are thus able to read others' emotions better (Herbert & Pollatos, 2012). Lower lAcc is associated with multiple mental health symptomatology, such as eating disorders, depersonalization and somatization (Pollatos *et al.*, 2008).

This variability in perceiving and understanding one's bodily signals affects one's ability to feel and know gender. Trans people cannot be expected to know their gender as quickly or in the same manner as cis people do,[4] since everyone feels their bodies in greater or lesser degrees.

A person listening to their heartbeats is not just perceiving their heart, there are sensations coming from the middle and inner ear, the pulses throughout the body, the skin, and more, which are internally and externally felt (Ádám, 1998). Ainley and colleagues believe they have found that when people with high IAcc focus attention on their heart rates, it lowers the precision of their interoception of other signals from their body, which therefore decreases the noise (Ainley *et al.*, 2016). Less noise opens the way for more accuracy for the sensation one is focusing attention on. It seems that if one region of the body is experiencing interference in processing, then the entire system has the presence of "noise" (Pollatos *et al.*, 2016).

Interoceptive noise can have two effects on gender perception. One hypothesis is that the interoceptive noise is the (incongruent) gendered sensations the individual needs to focus on to know their gender. The appearance of one's material body is not much help; it is sending feedback that is not matching how one feels on the inside. Only when one turns inward will the answers begin to reveal themselves. Second, this noise, when it is present, is a distraction from other attendant stimuli. Either the gender noise is so distracting that the person's ability to hear the rest of their bodily signals is reduced, or other bodily signals are so noisy that one cannot "hear" their gendered signals. The latter is particularly relevant when working with people who have experienced trauma (I will address this in Chapter 6). A trans person may become so overwhelmed by their gender trauma that to listen to

---

4   Cis is the commonly used prefix to indicate those people whose gender identity is congruent with the sex assigned at birth.

any of their interoception results in dissociation. This is a common clinical presentation. In Chapter 6, on trauma, there will be more discussion of dissociation. Internal and external factors can trigger a change in IAcc, such as physical changes (gender-affirming interventions) or psychological issues (stress related to pre-transition) or other situational contributors (Badoud & Tsakiris, 2017).

The problem of semiotics

According to Kandel (2012), "One cannot perceive that which one cannot classify" (p.287). Interoception is the self-perceiving of the self; my theory is that this internal level of perceiving oneself is a foundational source of how one comes to know one's gender. Body-schematics are the percepts a trans person must attune to in order to develop the self-awareness and thus self-knowledge of their transgender identity. There is no external feedback until the person begins to experiment with clothing, haircuts, prosthetics or binders/fillers. Here, though, I am talking about the time before experimentation, when the person is trying to figure out what these feelings are that will help them to know if they even need to experiment with their gender.

A "basic prerequisite of the normal functioning of the organism seems to be that interoceptive impulses should remain unconscious" (Ádám, 1998, p.182). This is the fundamental conundrum for trans people. These interoceptive processes want to remain non-conscious in nature, until they become unbearable (i.e. hunger or gender incongruence). Leder (1990) explores how the internal milieu remains recessive in order for the individual to focus and function through qualitative reduction, spatial ambiguity and spatiotemporal discontinuity.

The more dissociated or disconnected from their body someone is, the less likely they will be able to feel, recognize and label these sensations. Internal signals are the most elemental for understanding gender, particularly since the material body does not reinforce what the trans person feels of their self. Internal signals may also be a more accurate sense of self (Gallagher, 2005). The individual cannot rely on the visual of their body to tell them who they are and what their gender is; they must attune to the signals coming from inside themselves. The internal viscera are what will tell you if something in the visual field is not congruent. This is a displeasing sensation but has multiple, deeper layers. The desire to call up these non-conscious percepts is rubbing up against the design of our interoceptive systems. Our need to "detect, recognize, identify, discriminate" (Ádám, 1998, p.144) and label visceral changes is not a skill we have since it is not necessary for our survival unless there is an emergency in our system (hunger, thirst, gender). This is what Leder (1990) characterizes as the transition from the autonomy of "I can" (eat, drink, transition) to the "I must" that the visceral exerts on the self.

Visceral inputs do not have a clear semiotics. This is demonstrated by the dearth in visceral semiotics and by the reliance on unscientific, vague language (Ádám, 1998). For example, the Pennebaker Inventory of Limbic Languidness is a 54-item scale of physical symptoms; only one-third are interoceptive, the other two-thirds are exteroceptive and proprioceptive. Ádám (1998) stated that a viscerosensory vocabulary is theoretically possible but impractical since it would create so much cognitive noise for the individual. If general interoceptive sensations have little vocabulary, we have even less for internal gendered feelings (masculine or feminine are our only choices), which is why gender is so difficult to articulate.

When language becomes involved, it is woefully inadequate to capture this experience of self. It is a common refrain to hear trans people describe their search for gender by saying, "I had no language to express it" (Henry, 2017, p.96). This scant semiotics of gender is a burden on trans people who are required to verbally articulate their gender in order to be understood, recognized and allowed access to necessary medical interventions.

Many internal sensations are not able to be objectively measured, such as pain and shortness of breath (Parshall *et al.*, 2012). I count gender among them. There is another complication in expressing internal feelings. In a clinical setting, when we ask anyone to report their symptoms there is some distortion. This is what is called the labeling-as-distorting hypothesis (Ádám, 1998). As Ádám's research demonstrates, through the labeling-as-distorting hypothesis, as soon as you ask someone to vocalize their internal state, it has become corrupted. Language distorts the visceral information since it is primarily a non-conscious process. Labeling is an interpersonal endeavor; if we were alone, we would regulate ourselves without the need to label it. This is certainly a phase in a trans person's discovery when the individual finally knows their gender for themselves but is having difficulty labeling and explaining it to other people. Vygotsky (1981) theorized that cognition and verbalization could have formed distinct from each other during evolution and only by chance became interrelated through the pressure of social interaction. The social need to communicate necessitates shared language.

The stepsibling to "labeling-as-distorting" is response bias, which is particularly relevant to gender since there is so much social pressure related to it. Under the burden of societal expectations and transference, patients may be responding to our inquiries with what they think we (therapist or society) want to hear instead of their true feelings.

Core gender is the kernel of gender identity; the preverbal sense of oneself as a gendered being. The above evidence, of multiple interoceptive signaling happening in the body, the likelihood of many of those signals being endowed with a gendered feeling, and that they are resistant to language supports the definition of core gender. Part of my theory is that when the felt gender does not match the material body, this is experienced as a translation problem. This is part of the sensation of gender incongruence. There are sensory disconnects between the experienced gender and the body. Furthermore, there are the experienced gendered feelings that dysregulate interoceptive sensations and provoke the need for allostasis. It appears that there are different aspects of gender that reside within the body matrix, only some of which have been named. One example of felt sense dislocation is one's locomotion and sense of body changes when muscle density changes, either thickening with testosterone or softening with feminizing hormone treatment. These proprioceptive and interoceptive sensations feel more gender congruent, but most people cannot articulate it until after the change has happened. Additionally, our skin changes through hormone treatment. It feels different to the touch, and how the skin senses the world is modified through how the tissue changes. This can feel more gender congruent when it comes into alignment with one's experienced gender. It appears as if the relationship between physical sensation and gender identity is consistently reciprocal. What that feels like and why will be taken up later in this chapter, when we connect gender with the free energy principle, and in Chapter 2 which will consolidate gender with consciousness.

Research has shown that what little attentional energy we have is directed to exteroceptive percepts as adults; the opposite is true for infants, the exceptions being cases such as starvation or an urgency for bladder retention (Ádám, 1998; Broadbent, 1958; James, 1890/1950 (James said infants do not discriminate between internal and external)). Ádám (1998) said we could assume that the internal perceiving stops in early childhood, but the ability of feeling and labeling visceroceptive sensation is still possible since the neural circuitry is there. Knowledge of physical sensation is a result of the mix of visceral/somatic signals with memory, beliefs, illusions and "visceral hallucinations" (Ádám, 1998, p.77). It also seems in order to mentalize interoceptive signals, some interpersonal contact is necessary for the infant; that for the infant the other's body is just as essential in order to achieve homeostasis (Fotopoulou & Tsakiris, 2017). In Chapter 3, I will investigate early development and interactional forces in relation to gender.

The simplest form of wordless knowledge is the feeling of knowing (Damasio, 1999). He explains that the mind screens off things from itself. "One of the things the screen hides most effectively is the body" (Damasio, 1999, p.28). The feeling of knowing is not in conscious attention but running in the background, exerting a powerful influence (Damasio, 1999). This is true for gender as well. For most people it remains out of conscious awareness but is so foundational and powerful in the force it exerts on us.

Interoception is how humans receive the information to map the body to maintain homeostasis (Ainley *et al.*, 2016). Gender is part of that homeostatic information. Physical pain and skill (learning) are physicality features related to the musculoskeletal system. Mental pain is related to the internal milieu and viscera (Damasio, 2010).

The feeling of gender incongruence has roots in both mental and physical pain; when gender is dysregulated, there is a mental reaction to the physical components which are misaligned.

Higher interoceptive sensitivity is correlated with depth of experiencing of emotions (Wiens, 2005). This is further reinforced by Hohmann's (1966) research with subjects whose spinal cords were severed and who experienced a reduction in the feeling of emotions. This attests to what William James (1884) hypothesized more than a century ago, that one can feel emotions more deeply through the body.

Temperature stimuli within the body induce a feeling and provoke a need for action (Hua *et al.*, 2005). Craig (2015) calls this homeostatic emotion. There are two kinds of homeostasis: basic and sociocultural. Gender is subdivided in this same way. There is the basic (core) gender within the individual and interoception, and the sociocultural one that is more related to exteroception and how we are seen.

Emotional reactions engage basic homeostatic regulatory processes as well. Emotions are foundationally about homeostasis of the individual (Damasio, 2010). Gender becomes comprehensible through the perception of a feeling of dysregulation which needs an allostatic response (but cannot find one within the human system).

Free energy principle and why we do or do not feel our gender

What is the process when our gender equilibrium is dysregulated? How does this dysregulation occur? We can understand gender through our new understanding of how brains and bodies work. We previously believed that the body only sent afferent signals up and the brain processed them (without interpretation) directly but now we understand this process differently. Our brain is not a stimulus-response organ but an organ that is constantly producing hypotheses and explanations for the stimuli it receives (Seth & Friston, 2016). In the beginning of this century a new theory was produced called the free energy principle (FEP). The FEP is an information theory from computational neuroscience which attempts to explain how the brain seeks to conserve energy and recognize sensory information through predictive coding (Ainley *et al.*, 2016; Friston, 2009). Predictive coding is a process theory which proposes a schema of brain processes. This organizing principle of the brain is based on the Bayesian theorem from mathematics. This theorem lays out the process of revising the probability of a hypothesis based on prior knowledge of variables when new information is added to the mix. I will first explain the FEP more deeply and then show why it applies to gender.

Higher neuronal representations (in the brain) descend predictions (also called prior beliefs) to lower-level representations (afferent signals from the body) in what is called prediction error if there is a difference between the two. This mismatch moves up the chain and updates are made to the prior representations. As the information is exchanged through each level, the prediction error is settled through explanation of the sensory inputs or active inference (homeostatic or allostatic regulation; Seth & Friston, 2016). If no prediction error occurs, then no change is needed. Predictive coding theory reverses the historically common understanding of perception: that perception was only a bottom-up experience. Prediction errors are bottom-up/feedforward. They can be suppressed by predictions coming from the higher-level cortical representations. This is called perceptual inference, whereas taking an action to bring sensation to match the prediction is called active inference (Seth, 2013).

Top-down predictions create a set-point for homeostasis which primary interoceptive (afferent) signals can be measured against. This then provokes parasympathetic or sympathetic systems to act to return the system to stability through homeostasis or allostasis (Seth & Friston, 2016). Free energy is the quantity of prediction error within the system (Fotopoulou & Tsakiris, 2017). The brain learns how and where to direct attention in order to update its models from bottom-up prediction errors either to suppress errors or take action in relation to top-down predictions from its models. A balance is always being searched for between these two, in order to minimize surprise (free energy)[5] or, put another way, to optimize certainty. This balance is struck in part by the brain figuring out what are the more salient features to be focusing on in order to contextualize prediction errors or recalculate its predictions. Increasing the precision of predictions is therefore increasing one's interoceptive accuracy (lAcc; Fotopoulou & Tsakiris, 2017).

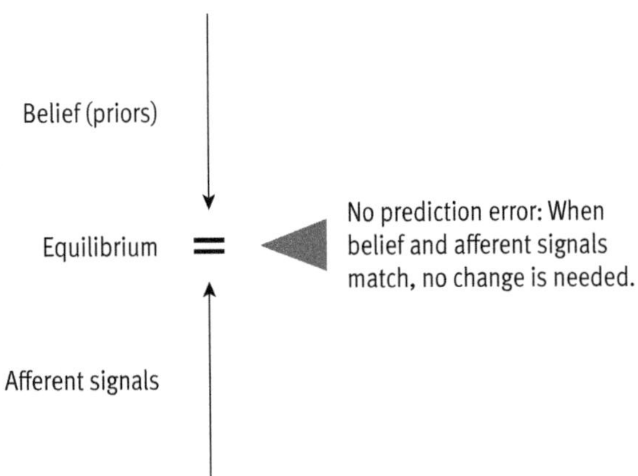

Figure 1.2 Model of predictive processing when no free energy occurs in cisgender experience

---

5   There are subtle differences between free energy and surprise, but that pulls us deeper into physics and Markov Blankets and for our purposes it is unnecessary. See Ramstead, Badcock & Friston (2018).

Probability distributions are used by the brain as the foundation of the prior beliefs that are present before sensory information reaches the brain. The brain processes the body as most probably being me (Apps & Tsakiris, 2014). These "beliefs" should be thought of as "neuronally encoded probability distributions" which are non-conscious (Seth & Friston, 2016, p.1). The qualities that define one's belief of their gender are the external states, sensations, actions and brain states. The latter two change to reduce, free energy/surprise or, as Duquette (2017) translates into psychotherapeutic jargon, uncertainty or fear. Think of the brain as having a top-down activation of (non-conscious) prediction (a prior belief) and a bottom-up activation of an interoceptive or exteroceptive stimulus. When the prior does not match the stimulus, there is surprise. The FEP proposes that the human system works to minimize the differences between the sensory experience and the internal models of the mind. Free energy is only reduced by increasing the accuracy between sensation and the prior either through action or suppression of prediction error through neuromodulator factors (i.e. change in expectation). The causes of the beliefs are obscured since they are inferred by sensory stimuli and are therefore "forever hidden behind a sensory veil" (Seth & Friston, 2016, p.2). Predictive coding appears implicated in the idea that subjective feelings are a result of the brain's predictions about interoceptive equilibrium (Seth, Suzuki & Critchley, 2012). Barrett, Quigley & Hamilton (2016) have a hypothesis that higher prediction error is correlated with inefficient allostasis.

The FEP explains why and how gender feels different for cis and trans people. Most cisgendered people are not aware of how they know their gender. They do not really feel it. They take it for granted that they are masculine/male or feminine/female. The feeling of their gender remains within the bounds of homeostasis. A cis man's brain predicts that his skin is tough and that he will sense his penis against his body; he expects to hear a certain tenor of voice and feel stubble on his face. The predictions match the afferent signals making their way up the chain to his cortex. However, for trans people the predictions do not match the afferent signals. A trans person's interoceptive/exteroceptive body signals are creating prediction errors when they come into contact with the brain's priors. Gender dissonance is free energy.

So why won't gender predictions change due to the consistent dissonance of the afferent signals? Because gender is a kind of hyperprior. Hyperpriors are a kind of prior that are possibly genetically encoded and cannot be resolved through homeostatic or allostatic capabilities of the body except in rare cases, under extreme stress (Clark, Watson & Friston, 2018). Therefore, gender is actually a hyperprior. It is not regulated through homeostasis or allostasis. Under the extreme stress of living in a transphobic society, with a material body that does not match the hyperprior, social reinforcement of the gender assigned at birth, conversion therapy and other constraining forces, the individual may consciously and/or unconsciously attempt to change (more accurately to suppress/repress) the gender hyperprior. This position is analogous to the defensive posture of denial. In my clinical experience the gender hyperprior is never changed; it lies in wait, running in the background until the person can acknowledge it.

When free energy occurs, change must occur to restore equilibrium: either bodily changes (active inference) or the prior predictions (perceptual inference). If any part of the system can change to reduce free energy than it will, whether that is the prior belief or efferent communication to the body to adjust the system to minimize surprise.

However, with gender, the change (transition) to minimize surprise must come from outside of the system.

So, a trans woman's brain has predictions of what her gender is—as feminine for instance—as it relates to the multiple aspects of her body and behavior. When new information is added, such as shaving her legs and how that feels and looks to her, the prior prediction for femininity may now fit the sensory information. Does this feel congruent or not through intero/exteroceptive pathways, (i.e. how it feels and how it looks)? The smooth look of the legs, the way the wind hits the skin differently, etc.

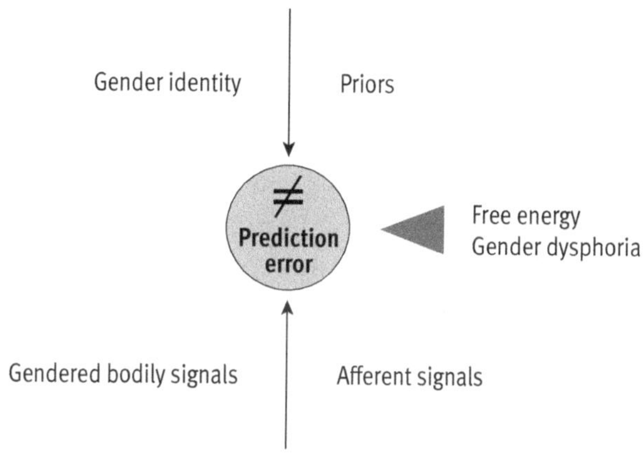

Figure 1.3 Model of free energy principle as it applies to transgender experience

Humans do not generally perceive their heart beats, the same way cis people do not feel their gender. This can be understood through predictive coding. When a stimulus is predicted, there is no need to update priors to match the incoming stimulus. Interoceptive and proprioceptive prediction errors can move in both directions. They can send signals to the brain to modify the prior beliefs or can take a top-down approach to make the priors a reality by changing one's actions (or reflexes) to come into alignment. No predictive errors between sensation and prior belief mean no updating and thus no perception of the stimulus (Ainley *et al.*, 2016). We know our heart should be beating so we do not need to be aware of or keep track of it. Applying this concept to gender, most people are not constantly aware of their gender. It is unnecessary for them to be, as there are no predictive errors occurring on a regular basis. However, for a trans person, the consistent prediction error and attempts to correct for it occupy the mind on conscious and unconscious levels.

For a trans person, each element of gender may or may not match the prediction or afferent signal. Prediction errors are the reaction to the interoceptive and exteroceptive signals that a trans person needs to allow themselves to feel in order to understand what the psycho-physical noise is inside them. They must connect to a process that is happening in a hundredth of a second and is non-conscious in nature. We know that gendered predictions cannot be changed. We must take the active inference path by taking action: be that hormones, shaving, binding, tucking, surgery, etc. For instance, a trans man (before hormone replacement therapy (HRT)) is receiving feminine interoceptive signals from his muscles or other internal viscera which are not predicted by his mind, thus creating free energy; but when he begins taking testosterone, that free energy disappears. My theory works to reinforce that the feeling of gender incongruence is not just a visual/auditory affair (what one looks and sounds like) but involves all our sensory information.

Thomas Page McBee in his memoir *Man Alive* sums up these interoceptive and proprioceptive changes that feel gender congruent and that he would not have been able to articulate specifically before they occurred in his body.

I didn't expect the visceral pleasure, either; the joy I found laying a hand on my rising pecs or lifting my shirt to study the hard center of my abs. I didn't expect the shift in my center of gravity or the calf muscles so big they brushed against my pants. I didn't expect the calm at the core of me, my strength a tactile feeling, cool and placid as a lake. (McBee, 2014, p.158)

This quote echoes what I hear in countless sessions with patients, McBee just puts it more poetically: this sensation of calm when free energy is reduced and gender stability is restored.

We know that trying to change someone's mind about their gender does not work (and is an illegal treatment to perform in some states and provinces). We have known it since some of the earliest descriptions of trans existence (Hirschfeld, 1919/1991). The prior expectations cannot be changed. Active inference is what is necessary in gender, bringing the body into alignment with the predictions. Just as applying psychotherapy to alter the mind not to register temperature is a preposterous proposal, so is applying it to change one's internal model of gender. The purpose of therapy is to aid in the connection to one's feelings and develop the ability to articulate and act on them.

The sense of body ownership comes from an integration in the brain of somatosensory afferent sensations (Tsakiris, 2010). The problem in Tsakiris' theory of body ownership is that he focuses on the visual being compared to the sensations and the mind accepting them as congruent or not. This is valid to a degree, but what I am proposing is that body ownership is not only about visual dissonance. Working from this hypothesis, an interesting study was done comparing cis women and trans men's sensory responses to their chest and hand being touched (Case et al., 2017). Subjects' responses were measured using magnetoencephalography (MEG). They found some differences in the trans men's MEG which indicated less body ownership of the breast (less response in the supramarginal gyrus and secondary somatosensory cortex) and higher emotional reaction (activity in the amygdala). This study affirms the differences in feeling about the body and leans towards the argument for the FEP, because the research method had participants with their eyes closed. It is not only about how one sees one's body but how one experiences the feeling of the body. The visual is important, but as stated earlier, the goal in this work is to highlight the other experiential aspects of gender.

A short explanation of the neuroscience of subjective feeling

Subjective feeling could be defined as the result of predictive inferences within the FEP (Seth, 2013). Feeling interoception does not determine emotions; it is the nature of the predictive signals which produce emotion (Seth *et al.*, 2012). The predictive signals related to gender for trans people result in the emotion usually called dysphoria. The nuclei of the periaqueductal gray (PAG) is where the workings of emotion are executed in the brain. The PAG may also be affecting signaling from the body. Our feeling of our feelings is implicated in this region of the brain along with the parabrachial nucleus (PBN) and the nucleus tractus solitaries (NTS). This is to illustrate that subjective feeling is a product of complex interaction of various regions of the brain and body. All the brain areas that receive body to brain stimuli also send signals back that influence the state of the body. This is called the resonant loop (Damasio, 2010).

Therefore, a feeling of an emotion is a "composite perception" of the mind and the body (Damasio, 2010, p.109).

Gender is then a composite of these composite perceptions. Within this resonant loop are continuous signals about our gendered feelings within the body. Our feelings are mainly coordinated through the insular cortex, which is implicated in representing and controlling visceral function and internal milieu (Damasio, 2010).

Pools of neurons processing stimuli based on one prediction model suppress other pools of neurons working on other models. Thus, perceptual experience results from the relative congruence of sensory input and the context it is happening in (Apps & Tsakiris, 2014). The theory goes that emotions are the result of movement in free energy: higher leading to more negative emotions and vice versa (Ainley *et al.*, 2016; Joffily & Coricelli, 2013).

The insula (in the bilateral, cluster peak BA 13) when studied with functional magnetic resonance imaging (fMRI) and heartbeat detection tests is associated with lAcc, and this BA 13 region has been associated with visceral perception.[6] This area of the insula is deemed the interoceptive cortex (Craig, 2003). The insula is assumed to be the place of integration of interoceptive sensations and the reconciling of predictive errors (Barrett & Simmons, 2015; Craig, 2009a; Menon & Uddin, 2010; Pollatos *et al.*, 2016). Optimizing for streamlined energy use, Craig (2015) proposes, is an evolutionary imperative that led to better and better interoceptive integration which in turn eventually produced subjective awareness. This precision of lAcc is transmitted by pyramidal cells (these cells are primarily responsible for electroencephalogram (EEG) signals) which are the ones that signal prediction error and correlate to a concentration of Gamma-Aminobutyric Acid (GABA) and Glutamate in the insula (Ernst *et al.*, 2013;

---

6   The insula is located deep in the cerebral cortex. One of its functions is awareness in the moment and subjective feeling. The bilateral, cluster peak BA 13 is the specific location of the insula in the brain.

Friston, 2009; Quattrocki & Friston, 2014). We will return to these brain areas in the next chapter and explore how interoception influences the development of the self.

Trans brains?

Brain research of trans people is still in its infancy. Through our exploration we should keep in mind that "our brains are as different as our faces" (Craig, 2015, p.251). I will quickly summarize what has been investigated so far in an effort to be diligent in providing context. Zubiaurre-Elorza's team (2013, 2014) studied cortical thickness pre- and post-hormone treatment and had only 29 and 42 trans subjects. Their study revealed that trans men have cortical thickness in between cis women and cis men and the converse is true for trans women; also, cortical thickness moved in the direction of the affirmed gender on hormone treatment. These results were similar to Luders and colleagues' (2012) study of pre-hormone treated trans women and Burke and colleagues (2017a), who found functional and structural changes on cortical thickness in areas related to body perception in trans men post-testosterone treatment. Post-hormone treatment has been shown to change brain volume further towards one's affirmed gender, albeit in a small sample of eight trans women and five trans men (Hulshoff Pol *et al.*, 2006). In adolescents, brain volume was similar overall in trans and cis groups, but in sex-dimorphic regions trans adolescents' brains looked slightly similar to their affirmed gender controls (Hoekzema *et al.*, 2015). Another study, which may have more clinical usefulness, found that testosterone treatment in trans men increased serotonin transporters (SERT) binding in the amygdala, caudate, putamen and median raphe nucleus and decreased it in trans women in the insula, anterior and midcingulate cortex, but estradiol aided in mitigating this SERT loss (Kranz *et al.*, 2015). SERT is a key aspect of the treatment of depression and anxiety. It is unclear if this is only changed due to testosterone or by other variables related to transition.

Hahn and colleagues (2014) studied functional and structural connectivity in 23 and 21 trans men and trans women respectively. Only trans women appeared to be inbetween the range of cis men and cis women on total intracranial volume (TIV) and both groups had a lower hemispheric connectivity ratio (HCR). However, a chapter in a recent neuroscience textbook shows that many of the studies are framed to look at the etiology of a "disease" to be diagnosed, and most with statistically insignificant sample sizes (Swaab & Bao, 2013).

Burke, Manzouri and Savic (2017b) studied 40 trans men and 27 trans women using fractional anisotropy (FA) to measure white matter connections and found sex-atypical FA-values in the right inferior fronto-occipital tract. This area of the brain is believed to mediate own-body perception. Therefore, they interpreted their results as possible signs of the incongruity between self-perception and one's body (Burke *et al.*, 2017b). This result is not conclusive as there are large-scale networks in the brain associated with one's sense of body ownership and the psychological processes that go with it.

Feusner and colleagues (2016), in a study of 27 trans men prior to testosterone treatment, compared them to heterosexual cis men and cis women on viewing a body-morphing visual task. Subjects viewed images of their body morphing from female to gender ambiguous to male. The trans men had weaker functional connections in the anterior cingulate cortex (ACC) and precuneus/posterior cingulated cortex (PCC) region of the default mode network (DMN), and covariation in the left pregenual anterior cingulate cortex (pACC) in the DMN during longer viewing durations. The DMN is known to be involved in self-referential thinking, which is why the researchers interpreted their findings as pointing towards feelings of gender dysphoria being related to self-reflective thinking, as opposed to being self-reflexive. Self-reflexive would be characterized more by the salience network and one's interoceptive system. They believe this activity in the pACC is because of top-down modulation from the DMN on the salience network. This is suggestive of free energy principles.

In a similar study, Manzouri, Kosidou and Savic (2015) found in 28 trans men weaker connections to the EBA, fusiform cortex and posterior cingulate as well as in the pACC, precuneus, thalamus and left temporoparietal junction (TPJ) to those regions when viewing morphed bodies and asked to state: "To what degree is this picture you?" Their TPJ connections were stronger to the left inferior and middle frontal gyri. This appears to the researchers as unique cortical midline structures and weaker connections to the body ownership perception networks in trans men. With a similar sample, Burke and colleagues (2017a) had similar results. One other interesting study found higher connectivity and centrality in the primary somatosensory cortex, superior parietal lobule, and visual and auditory regions in trans subjects, which seems to suggest that these individuals had higher activity of sensory input related to body representation (Lin *et al.*, 2014).

These studies are framing the research questions from a theory of gender as sex dimorphic[7] which may not capture the complexity of gender. Even if we see differences between trans and cis subjects, the sample sizes are very

---

7   See *Brain Storm: The Flaws in the Science of Sex Difference* by Rebecca Jordan-Young (2011) for a full critique of all brain sex dimorphic research.

small and do not account for variations within each group. This work offers interesting glimpses into the brain but does not offer concrete conclusions to the researchers' questions. Their results are correlative but not causative. A 2015 study supports my thinking that brains are not sex dimorphic: Joel and colleagues (2015) analyzed MRIs of more than 1400 brains along sex dimorphic features. They found that male and female brains have immense overlap in all regions, grey matter, white matter and connections, leading them to conclude that brains cannot be categorized as male or female and we need to recognize the "variability of human brains mosaic" (p.5).

When discussing some of the trans brain studies, it is also worth noting the language and framing of the trans people in the literature. The cisgender subjects are generally referred to as "healthy" controls; this reveals a bias towards a disease model mindset. Additionally, sexual orientation is being studied alongside gender identity, but the sexual orientation of the trans people was determined using their sex assigned at birth, which seems to show a lack of recognition of the separation of sexual orientation, especially when the work of Blanchard,[8] is used to discuss it in the Manzouri and colleagues (2015) study. This also reveals a view of trans people by the researchers which does not recognize their subjects' affirmed gender (i.e. calling trans men who are attracted to women homosexual). Additionally, many of these studies are operationalizing gender and sexual orientation as binary. Clearly more research is needed with research questions that include the input of trans, genderqueer, and non-binary identified people.

---

8   See Serano (2010) for a solid summary of pathologization of trans women by Blanchard.

A precise self

Precision refers to the reliability of the signal in which the brain is predicting the cause and context of the stimuli. Thus, the prediction errors with high precision have access to higher-level hierarchies and can update higher-level predictions (Seth & Friston, 2016). This is based on the model that Ainsley and colleagues (2014) propose as the understanding of lower IAcc and certain clinical presentations such as alexithymia where the mind has a precise prior and the interoceptive signals do not meet the expectation. We know that free energy can be reduced in two ways: by changing the perception of the prior belief (which we know does not work for gender— you cannot change someone's experienced gender) or by taking action (which we know does work for most people, i.e. social/medical transition). Through applying the FEP to gender, we can extrapolate why social/medical interventions work to relieve the suffering of trans people.

This integration of efferent and afferent interoceptive signals contributes to the feeling of a self (Seth, Suzuki & Critchley, 2012). The explanation that these sensory inputs add up to a self is the most economical understanding when it comes to minimizing the free energy (Apps & Tsakiris, 2014). For instance, my face becomes more recognizable as my face because it is the one that is usually looking back at me when I am in front of a mirror. It has a high probability of happening, so has a high prior prediction and thus low prediction error. Apps and Tsakiris suggest that every sensory process can contribute to self-recognition (2014). They go on to argue that the FEP explains the process of self-recognition. Aspects of one's body will be recognized as part of the self through predictions in exteroceptive sensations being congruent with interoceptive sensory information. The self-recognition is accomplished through this integration. They also propose through a review of relevant literature that there are three areas of the brain engaged in self-recognition (process the surprise that is triggered): the middle frontal gyrus, the intraparietal sulcus and the anterior insula. Thinking mathematically, lower entropy is what the brain needs to resist disorder; entropy is surprise averaged overall (Friston, 2007).

The FEP corresponds well with the experience within the body of the individual who has participated in a gendered medical intervention or used a prosthetic or DIY gender modifications with their body. For instance, for some trans women, the feeling and appearance of their body without male genitalia is not a sensation they need to accommodate for after surgery; it already feels natural. The probabilistic representation of a "flatness" in their genital area has been present in their mind all along; there is no surprise, no need to update the prior, and thus low entropy. There is a certain "click" in the brain when a person binds his chest for the first time and he feels its correctness. The sensory inputs finally match the top-down prediction and one can recognize the self in that moment without effort. For instance, the patients I have worked with who have had masculinizing chest surgery have all instantly felt interoceptively and visually that their bodies were being returned to them in the proper form, regardless of how they identified: trans, trans man, man, genderqueer, butch lesbian, etc. The identity did not lead their need, their bodies did.

It is possible that the FEP could explain the interesting result of Keo-Meier and colleagues' (2014) Minnesota Multiphasic Personality Inventory (MMPI) study in the U.S.A. They administered the MMPI to trans men before initiation of testosterone, with cis men and cis women as controls (the MMPI is scored according to gender; Keo-Meier has a 2016 follow-up article addressing this issue). Then they administered it again to all participants after three months, the trans men had been on testoste-rone for that time period. The degree of psychopathy (depression, psychasthenia, hysteria, paranoia) drastically reduced as a result of the testosterone in only three months. The MMPI is a reliably static personality test that does not really change over time, which is what makes these results so important. There are no visible physical changes in the first three months of testosterone treatment. Therefore, these results are not because of body-image changes or gender recognition in public. Oda and Kinoshita (2017) in Japan found similar results of improved mental health with testosterone for trans men. I do not think it can be explained by the relief of the decision-making process being over; the profound psychic improvement in MMPI scores must be due to a psychic/physical change more foundational than just relief. There must be some non-conscious visceral intero/proprioceptive changes happening which are bringing psychophysical equilibrium to the individual. It may be what Kranz and colleagues (2015) found in their study discussed earlier where SERT binding increased for trans men on testosterone for one to four months, in some way acting in an anti-depressant/anti-anxiety manner. We cannot say for certain unless we combine the methods of both studies. Following my line of thinking, I believe that much of the internal noise of gender dissonance is being turned down. The free energy is minimized, which is improving mental well-being because one is approaching one's optimal gender equilibrium.

I believe the same phenomenon exists for trans women when they begin hormone treatment, from my clinical experience (yet to be validated by research) and captured by this trans woman's words:

> Oestrogen became the food for my brain. I remember one of the first times I ventured out walking by myself. It felt so natural and so real I never wanted it to end. I broke down and cried because I had never felt so alive before. It was pure ecstasy. (Henry, 2017, p.28)

The feeling of what's missing

The presence of phantom limb sensation is a common experience of amputees. This was discovered during the American Civil War when a tremendous number of amputations were performed and William James studied the soldiers' experiences post-surgery (1887). It is the experience of feeling sensation (many times pain but other sensations too) from a part of the body that no longer exists. It is common medical knowledge now that most amputees will experience some phantom sensation. Despite its prevalence, one older survey of American veterans found that although 61 percent reported to their doctor phantom pain, only 17 percent were referred for treatment. The remaining 44 percent were labeled mentally ill (Sherman & Sherman, 1983). This is not too dissimilar to trans people's experiences of many health care professionals who do not believe their subjective experiences of their own bodies.

There is also the phenomenon of aplasic phantom sensation, which is phantom feeling of a body part that a person was born without due to birth defect. This was not known until 1961 when the first study of young people born without at least one of their limbs was conducted at two hospitals in the Bronx, New York (Weinstein & Sersen, 1961). They asked subjects aged 5 to 25 years old if they too had experienced phantoms. They found that 5 out of the 30 had a phantom. Interestingly, the parents of the children were aware that phantom sensation existed but had never asked their child if they experienced one.

Aplasic phantom experiencers do not usually report feeling the phantom until between the ages of five and eight (Gallagher, 2005; Gallagher and Meltzoff, 1996). Researchers believe it takes until these ages because the child needs time to develop language to articulate their experience before they can report it. This is strikingly similar to the experience of trans youth (and adults) who also require time to understand their own sensations and then be able to verbally report it. How some trans men experience a missing penis or trans women experience missing breasts or hips can be understood as aplasic phantoms. I believe the variability in IAcc contributes to this delay in a trans person's ability to feel, understand and articulate how all those percepts add up to gender.

Ramachandran proposes that we have a hard-wired body map at birth (Ramachandran & Blakeslee, 1998). There are two maps of the body in the brain, according to him: the one from birth and the one that is continuously receiving signals from the current state of the body. He believes that all our body is a phantom, constructed moment by moment by the brain's organization of all the sensations running up to it. However, we do know that the periphery, spinal cord and brain using various mechanisms are involved in generating phantoms (Nikolajsen & Staehelin Jensen, 2001).

Furthermore, a small research study and my clinical experience support the fact that trans people experience phantom sensations of gendered "missing" body parts (Langer, 2014; Ramachandran & McGeoch, 2008). Phantoms can be useful to amputees in order to help animate their prosthetics, in Chapter 5 I will discuss this utility for trans experience and sexual functioning.

The phantoms prove both variety of the body matrix and how our brains experience gender. Ramachandran (Ramachandran & Blakeslee, 1998) has a curious view on pain from his work with phantom pain. He believes that pain is an opinion on the internal condition of the person, not just a reaction to injury, because there is no direct link between nociceptors (pain neuroreceptors) and so-called pain centers in the brain. There is so much interplay between other areas of the brain and sensory levels that perceptions are not so direct. The pain of gender dysphoria relates well to this theory. The individual's sense of dissonance is an opinion about one's gender equilibrium. Opinion can be a dangerous word since medical opinion has been of the opinion that a person's opinion about their gender is less valid than chromosomal or visual genital evidence. Nonetheless, this frame that the brain is making a judgment about the state of being which results in a sense of pain has relevance for gender dysphoria and relates well to the FEP. When the dissonance is reduced, a foundational sense of mental well-being is achieved by the individual, profoundly, instantaneously, dramatically when it comes to transition-related interventions. At the body level, balance is accomplished.

Knowing and being one's gender in solitude

Anxiety comes from "not being able to orient yourself in your own existence" (May, 1975, p.58). Inquiry into the self requires reflection, introspection and perception (Gallagher, 2011). The perceptual skill of interoception is believed to be essential to emotional self-regulation (Craig, 2009a; Herbert & Pollatos, 2012). Knowing one's self also requires physical courage which demands one to listen to and be sensitive to one's body (May, 1975). This trifold approach is what is needed to deeply understand one's gender. The first two are the methods employed and discussed the most in the literature, but the technique and action of perception is more likely ignored. We need to remember that "exteroception inhibits interoception" (Ádám, 1998, p.89). Some of the other causes for interoceptive dysfunction could be that the afferent signals themselves, or our perception of the afferent signals are incorrect, or our predictions are incorrect (Duquette, 2017).

Introspection is a cornerstone of psychodynamic psychotherapy but this has its limitations when it comes to the body. As the above theories demonstrate, there is a circular causality in relation to mind/body interaction which allows for psychotherapeutic intervention (Duquette, 2017). As psychotherapists, we can only really engage with our patients through verbal inquiry. Therapists need patients to experiment with their bodies outside the consulting room and report back to us. Creative arts therapists have an advantage over exclusively talk therapists in that they can accompany the patient in embodied activities such as movement/dance, music, and working with the more visceral arts materials such as clay, wax, woodworking, etc. Trans patients need to be encouraged to use their bodies with awareness. Then, with an attuned therapist, they can do the work of interpreting the signals.

We need to help patients feel comfortable to talk without knowing. The treatment room is the place in the world where we can speak before we actually know what we are saying or meaning. Both therapist and patient need to be able to tolerate the ambiguity of the situation or the patient's certainty. (In talking with other clinicians new to working with gender, common complaints/fears are that the patient is "going too fast" or "obsessed with transitioning" (certainty) or that the therapist interprets exploration of gender (ambivalence) as proof of the patient "not really being trans." Both scenarios create a catch 22 for trans patients in therapy with unskilled clinicians that no matter where they are in the process, they will be pathologized for it.)

The direction of the treatment requires us to provoke and transmit the ability to tune into one's interoceptive feelings. There is precedent for this in physiology. Ádám (1998) could teach patients to feel a previously non-conscious visceral feeling. He inserted a stimulating device into the small intestines of subjects. The device would be activated while subjects were attached to an EEG which would measure their brain activity to the stimulus. This way one could measure response to the stimulus that was out of conscious awareness. At certain levels the EEG would register the stimulation, but the subject consciously reported no sensation but did state mood changes. This intestinal stimulation affected the subjects' mood non-consciously. Furthermore, in an even more remarkable turn, he was able to verbally train subjects to consciously feel the visceral stimulation at levels which were initially completely non-conscious. He did this by beginning with stimulation at levels that reached consciousness and worked his way down to lower thresholds while alerting the subject that the stimulus was about to happen. This is conditional learning. Interoception has some kind of memory (something can be learned, adaptation can occur for example when we are toilet trained).

Psychotherapists obviously cannot implant electrodes to provoke gendered feelings. However, we can start with exploring the gendered aspect of the patient's body or social interactions which are most uncomfortable and obvious to them, then slowly connect to other gender elements that may have more subtle signals. Many patients have begun inquiry about their gender with "I don't like my chest and it feels uncomfortable when people call me miss." Then commences the process of understanding the meaning of those elements for the patient and experimentation to see how the alternatives fit. Usually that leads us to other elements of body and behavior and into submerged and subtle aspects of their being in a gender. In perceiving unconscious material, Lawrence (1948) found that it was easier to teach subjects to perceive small percepts if you started with larger ones first and worked progressively down to the smaller differences.

It may not be an electrode but suggesting experimentation with clothing or prosthetics can feel quite electric the first times one puts on a dress or a prosthetic penis. Being able to process that jolt and make sense of it in therapy provides a powerful signal of one's gender. Many times, the process includes teasing apart internalized transphobia, shame and other judgments to find the core gender feelings. We will plunge into shame and internalized transphobia in subsequent chapters.

If the patient is not ready for that leap into gender-affirming experimentation, an alternative is through recommending activities with their body such as dancing, yoga or sport. This is an intervention which I employ with anyone exploring their gender (or trauma), to try to find some physical activity in which they can enjoy their body. Once able to enjoy their body in an ungendered way, it helps them connect in more complicated gendered ways. There is some interoceptive research which supports why this works. Lower IAcc people have a lower habitual salience for this sensory process (Ainley *et al.*, 2016). Subjects with low IAcc can improve their sensitivity by doing other "stressful" physical activities such as exercise or salient emotional reaction, as opposed to connecting to endogenous signals (Ádám, 1998). Engaging in a bodily task that increases your interoceptive signals helps you to feel them and identify them. If your heart rate is higher from running, it is easier to perceive it. It also helps you self-regulate (Herbert & Pollatos, 2012).

Another bodily activity with even less physical restraints (particularly for patients who have difficulty with movement) is meditation and mindfulness. Mindfulness training is found to increase interoceptive awareness and sensitivity (Domschke *et al.*, 2010; Farb, Segal & Anderson, 2013; Norman *et al.*, 2012). Mindfulness body scan training over eight weeks has demonstrated some improvement in IAcc (Fischer, Messner & Pollatos, 2017). Research also supports that people with higher IAcc may be able to tap into their intuition more when making decisions (Dunn *et al.*, 2010; Pollatos *et al.*, 2012). If one is to transition, then decision making which is located within the subject is essential.

Psychopathology complicates the picture for some trans people who may struggle with mental health. Those people with depression have lower IAcc, whereas those with anxiety usually have higher interoceptive sensitivity which can result in lower IAcc (related to being overly aware of signals which increases one's vulnerability to anxiety; Domschke *et al.*, 2010; Garfinkel and Critchley, 2013; Paulus & Stein, 2010; Pollatos, Traut-Mattausch & Schandry, 2009). In a 2013 study of people with major depressive disorder, Furman and colleagues found that those with depression have lower IAcc and that this reduced the individual's ability to connect to and use their interoceptive signals in decision making (as well as to feel positive arousal). Approaching the world with a bias towards feeling threatened or a negative self-view leads the mind to interpret afferent signals through those lenses, therefore inaccurately. The prediction error then leads those with depression to withdraw or those with anxiety to avoid (Paulus & Stein, 2010). The researchers coined the term "misinteroception" for this phenomenon. Similarly, Kawaguchi and colleagues (2016) found erroneous interpretation of bodily signals (as a threat) in social anxiety disorder. Therapists will do well to notice and intervene on the observable aspects of interoception, such as breath, facial expressions, posture, voice, eye contact, bodily movements (Duquette, 2017). One intervention to reduce anxiety in the moment is slowing down the breath (Zautra *et al.*, 2010). We can have patients purposefully putting both their feet on the ground to stimulate proprioceptors (Craig, 2011). The complications of depression and anxiety on IAcc alone demonstrate how it may take someone with mental health concerns longer to know their gender than someone without a diagnosis.

In conclusion, the above described processes of being and knowing are the subtle physical and psychological processes through which one can discover their own gender (with or without a therapist). I am firmly locating gender within the individual, as a primarily subjective experience. Our position as a therapist is not to know anything for the patient or predict anything or to tell anything. We are there to create a Winnicottian "potential space" for our patients to feel the many aspects of gender in their bodies, tolerate the ambiguity and create the best expression of those feelings.

Rollo May (1975) deftly explains how creative insight works in art and psychotherapy. He explains that creative insight does not just occur because it is right or true or even helpful, but because it completes some form which until that point was unfinished within the self. It is why we always seem to ask "How did we not see it sooner?", to which the answer is: "We were not psychologically ready yet." Every therapist has experienced this: that an insight they have offered to the patient does not "hit" the patient until weeks, months, years later (and is usually offered again by someone other than the therapist much to our frustration that the patient could "hear" it from someone else and not us).

The creative impulse (for our purposes: gendered feelings) is conveying something from our preconscious and unconscious which is not a part of rationality or outside control (May, 1975). Therefore, someone cannot solely think their way through it. They have to practice being before they can know it. Sometimes that being comes through one's dreams, like Leo from *Trans Voices*: "I used to see myself as a boy in my dreams and imagination. I wished I could be born again or that I would just wake up one morning realising that I had turned into a boy" (Henry, 2017, p.20).

Polanyi (1958) rejected the idea of objective scientific detachment in his book *Personal Knowledge*. He understood that knowledge needed to include the "hidden reality," which was no less objective. This is what I establish here: that knowing gender must come from feeling and comprehending what is usually hidden (tacitly known in Polanyi's words) but is still objective fact.

Through the principles and clinical experiences set up here, I am leading the reader to the understanding that being and knowing one's gender is not a decision. It is an act of acceptance of what is true. It is a recognition of what the mind/body already know about itself but which resists being captured by language. The decision about what to do with that knowledge will be tackled in the following chapters.

CHAPTER 2

Foundations of Consciousness and Gender

How does the individual discriminate between sensory stimuli? And how does one integrate this information and know how to react to it (Chalmers, 2002)? These are the same questions which we are fundamentally asking when we ask someone about their gender. As Chalmers points out, the harder question is how does this physical process in the brain become subjectivity? This is what we encounter when we confront gender. How does this body and/or brain produce a subjective experience that is unrecognizable to the outside observer? In trans experience, one's public/external body is mis/recognized by the other, with the private experience disbelieved by everyone, including the subject.

Philosopher Frank Jackson (1982), in his argument against physicalism, states that there are perceptions and sensations that cannot be completely known through physical information. This unexplainable phenomenon is known as qualia. Qualia do not cause anything physical on their own even though something physical is causing *them*. He illustrates the nature of qualia with two analogies. In the first, a man named Fred has a higher perception of color vision than other humans do. He can see differing qualities of red in a batch of tomatoes. When asked, he can consistently sort the tomatoes into two categories, even after they are mixed together again while he is blindfolded. He calls them red1 and red2 since our language does not completely capture that what he is perceiving are in fact two different colors—our restricted understanding and language are all that exist.

Even if science could discover how Fred's rods and cones were different than those of other humans so that he is able to have these perceptions, we still would not know *what it was like for him* to experience these colors. The physical information alone does not grant us access to knowing his experience. The phenomenal features of the effects of this mental state are qualia. We simply cannot know what it is like to be Fred.

Jackson (1982) also proposed this analogy in the understanding of consciousness. Imagine that there is a neuroscientist in the future who is an internationally recognized leader in the neuroscience of color vision. She has only ever lived in a black and white visual world, never seeing any other colors. She has knowledge of all the physical processes of color. This allows her to understand the easy problems such as how we discriminate stimuli to then integrate it and identify the color or the process of what color names go with which wavelengths on the light spectrum. However, the hard problem she has is not knowing what it is like to experience the color blue. There are physical facts about how the brain functions which do not tell us what we want to know about the nature of consciousness (Chalmers, 2002; Jackson, 1982).

Understanding gender is quite similar to Jackson's examples. International experts in transgender health have historically understood that the phenomenon of trans identity exists but not how or where it exists. And more importantly what the internal sensation feels like to be transgender (unless they are trans themselves).

They have found solutions to the body problems through endocrinology and surgery. They know how testosterone or estrogen physically affect the body in order to bring the emotional and physical suffering to an end. Surgeons continue to advance the intricacies of what biologically needs to be harnessed and fashioned to shape the body to functional and aesthetic experienced gender, which nerves need to be connected to provide the possibility of orgasm or which millimeter of bone needs to be shaved for a more feminine profile. Unless they are transgender though, they cannot know what it actually feels like to embody that space.

The fact remains that the conscious experience of being transgender is not the same as comprehending the biology of gender or the psychology of gendered behavior. Cisgender people know what *their gender* feels like and can experience some aspects of gender expression, but not the internal embodiment of transness. It is only in the last few decades that trans writers, researchers and clinicians have been studying and furthering our understanding of being transgender. Gender affirmative surgeries and hormone treatment do not solely make someone masculine or feminine, it is their consciousness that embodies that transformation that completes the resonant loop of gender. Cis people often do not understand this, since if they were exposed to those interventions, it would feel awful to them to experience those gendered transformations. Additionally, hormones or surgery would not alter their experienced gender. This is because they would be basing it on their own subjectivity, their own consciousness. The qualia of the conscious experience of being transgender is the further aim of this chapter.

Ramachandran locates neuroscience today to be in the phenomenon-driven stage, still searching for the basic laws, not quite at the theory-driven stage (Ramanchandran

& Blakeslee, 1998). Gender is on that same cusp. I have attempted here to flesh out the phenomenology of transgender in order to advance our understanding of gender in general. My goal is to locate transgender within the gender spectrum, not as an exceptional gender. Essential to this objective is the localizing of gender as an aspect of consciousness.

Consciousness resists categorization as a mental or physical phenomenon (Searles, 1997). We have neither the access nor the means to objectively measure mental states (Damasio, 2010). This is where the split occurs between the "old guard," those who have studied the phenomenon of transgender, and the "new guard," those who include academics in Trans Studies, which distinguishes itself by including the embodied subjective experience of the subject into their clinical work with trans communities. The new (avant) guard of clinicians rejects the medicalization of gendered experience and professionals who do not presume to know another's gender. It echoes Searles: "I am conscious regardless of what anybody else thinks" (1997, p.15). I am my gender, no matter what anyone else thinks.

Gender is observable by others in only two of its three manifestations: the visual representation that includes the shape of the body, and the behavior of the individual (embodiment). Experiential gender can only be known by the subject. Gender is a composite experience of these three. Consciousness is a composite experience as well. The mind collects images of all interoceptive and exteroceptive percepts coming through the body through brain maps. Damasio (2010) uses the word images to reflect all sensory information, not just visual information. These images are only available to the mind in which they occurred. These brain maps take three forms: visual, auditory and somatic. This information is stacked in such a way that one aspect is always related to the other two sensory experiences, which facilitates integration. This integration is relevant to the process of feeling gender incongruence. If these maps are not lining up in some way, then free energy occurs for the individual, creating that feeling of dissonance. The brain does more than map body states; it changes them and can even conjure up states which have not happened yet (Damasio, 2010). The visual, auditory and somatic forms of consciousness are the same structure as gender; however only the visual and auditory can be experienced by others.

The understanding of gender and consciousness do not fit neatly into either a physical or mental space. Both are qualitative subjective experiences and simultaneously part of the natural physical realm. There is an evidential gap between our first-person subjective introspection and scientifically measured brain events (Damasio, 2010). As opposed to a thing, consciousness is practically a process (Edelman, 2004). It is an embodied phenomenon: simultaneously a physical property of the natural world and a subjective mental apparatus. This is a rejection of both dualism and materialism (Searles, 1997). Consciousness is an "inner, first-person, qualitative phenomenon" (Searles, 1997, p.5). This definition succinctly captures gender identity as well. The fact that consciousness does not fit neatly into a discrete category makes duelists nervous. We could say the same about gender. It is not a static entity; it is a dynamic process running throughout our beings. Gender does not only reside in certain areas of our bodies, brains, or minds; gender is everywhere and nowhere. It is both physical and mental. It is non-binary but comes in shades from multiple aspects of our bodies. These facts make people fearful, nervous, angry, homicidal (high rates of violence/harassment/abuse against trans people) and suicidal (James *et al.*, 2016). The search for an etiology of trans experience in brain scans is not taking the full picture into account, that gender is more complex than a single neurological process or discrete brain area. Our brains react to a singular experience in different areas of the brain simultaneously (Damasio, 2010).

Just as we cannot isolate exactly where consciousness comes from in the brain, neither can we dissect gender in the brain. Mental life is the result of neurons increasing or decreasing their firing behavior (Searles, 1997). Crick (1994) says our complex sensations of consciousness are emergent properties of the activity of interaction between many parts of the brain. Gender could be easily classified as a set of complex sensations and, to follow Crick, it is also an emergent property as the result of activity in various parts of our brains.

Our burgeoning consciousness is based in our bodies. Even our in-utero experience is the basis for mapping out qualia. This mapping is what all other external signaling will be based on (Edelman, 2004). Even though we would not say people are only their embodiment, we could say "the continuity of the first-person perspective provided by that embodiment is what makes them persons" (Radden, 2011, p.549). If we are talking about embodiment, then we are also talking about gender. The definition of that gender is quite individual. This is not a gender essentialist position in the traditional form (i.e. masculinity/femininity linked to genital presentation and chromosomes). But a position that the form gender can take is any masculine or feminine shape, regardless of the body. However, the expression of that unique shape *is* essential to the survival of the individual. The internal core gender is what is essential and determines the direction of expression to achieve equilibrium.

The concept of presence is understood across disciplines as one's subjective sense of reality and self in the world and is the experience of healthy conscious experience (Seth *et al.*, 2012). Presence could be one of the structural properties of consciousness (Seth, 2009). Presence occurs as a result of interoceptive signals matching predictions, which results in low prediction error in a body–brain–environment flexible loop (Seth *et al.*, 2012). The sentient self is an integration of emotional and bodily representations in context at every moment in time through the anterior insular cortex (AIC; Craig, 2009b). One's gender presence is unique and individually essential. In order to accomplish presence for many trans and gender diverse people, some tangible intervention is needed: clothes, haircut, hormones, surgery, etc.

Consciousness, self and gender

The creation of a self is only possible because of the brain's ability to map and represent the body in the mind (Damasio, 2010). Evolutionarily, consciousness is oriented towards homeostasis. As I have been arguing, the search for gender congruence is equally directed towards the reduction of tension within the individual. Utilizing Damasio's structure of how consciousness and self develop, I will demonstrate how gender is foundationally emergent within these structures. Damasio's theory is a topographical one: proto-self to core self to autobiographical self.

The proto-self is constructed by body-mapping. This unbreakable body loop is present from early childhood (Damasio, 2010). The fulcrum of consciousness is the proto-self; consciousness begins its existence in this form. The proto-self consists primarily of interoceptive signals. This integration takes place at the brainstem level (old brain), specifically in the nucleus tractus solitaries (NTS), parabrachial nucleus (PBN is a complementary homeostatic sensory region), periaqueductal gray (PAG is the homeo-static motor region), area postrema, hypothalamus and superior colliculus (deep layers). At the cerebral cortex (evolutionarily new brain) level, interoceptive integration occurs within the insular cortex, anterior cingulate cortex and exteroceptive portals from the frontal eye fields (BA 8) and the somatosensory cortices.

NTS PBN PAG Area postrema Hypothalamus Superior colliculus Insular cortex Anterior cingulate cortex	All interoceptive integrative areas (integrating areas from within the body)	Areas related to core gender
Frontal eye fields (BA 8) Somatosensory cortices	External sensory areas (from outside the body)	

Figure 2.1 Proto-self (core gender)
(Adapted from Damasio, 2010)

These neural patterns are integrated into body maps. These maps include "master interoceptive maps, master organism maps and maps of the externally directed sensory portals" (Damasio, 2010, p.190). The insular cortex seems to be the place of integration for interoceptive and exteroceptive integration and particularly implicated is the AIC in the processing of interoception, visceral representations and emotions (Craig, 2009b; Craig, 2015; Seth *et al.*, 2012). The processing path for the interoceptive cortex runs from the posterior insula to the mid-insula to the AIC and is central to consciousness (Craig, 2009b, 2015). Bodily sensations occur in the mid-insula but emotional feelings happen in the AIC (Craig, 2015). The insula is thought to be involved in decision making and how the mind encodes bodily changes (Ainley *et al.*, 2016).

The posteromedial cortices appear to be at the intersection of the interoceptive, proprioceptive and exteroceptive systems as an integrator of these systems (Damasio, 2010). Interoception, exteroception and cognitive functioning all activate distinct regions of the insula in highly specific ways (Simmons *et al.*, 2013). Damasio (2010) hypothesizes that this area plays a part in consciousness as the interplay between background and foreground of the self.

As discussed in Chapter 1, the sensations of gender identity, one's core gender (in the body matrix), consist primarily of the interoceptive signals from the body, with a segment coming from the exteroceptive visual field. My premise is that core gender begins in the proto-self, and its primary construction is based on interoceptive integration. These images of the body generate what Damasio calls primordial feelings which precede all other feeling and are the first moments of subjectivity (Damasio, 2010). Primordial feelings are *the how and the what* that our body matrix is built from. The integration is what produces the feeling of an emotion (Craig, 2015). All these images of the self and non-self collected together produce the conscious mind (Damasio, 2010).

This foundational sense of self is almost exclusively generated by our internal percepts, which situates core gender identity in the proto-self. Our primordial feelings are the basis of our feelings which make up our unarticulated gender identity. This composition of the proto-self reinforces my theory that interoceptive percepts are intrinsically linked with gender.

One's sense of being is built on the signals from the internal milieu, visceral and vestibular signaling. The proto-self maps the many dimensions of the body, but it does not perceive or carry knowledge of it (Damasio, 1999). I propose that kernels of gender identity are a part of the non-conscious proto-self. Core gender is a part of lower-order consciousness.

Awareness in the proto-self gives rise to primordial feelings. Without language, the primordial feelings of the body are understood in the mind as knowing that my body exists in the present tense independent of others/objects (Damasio, 2010). This is not yet the interpersonal experience of a self but purely intrapsychic experience. Damasio (2010) notes: "The simple self at the bottom of the mind is a lot like music but not yet poetry" (p.186). There is a rhythm but no specific articulation yet. Damasio (2010) also says: "All feelings of emotion are complex musical variations on primordial feelings" (p.21). The primordial feelings of gender are a foundational part of that musical variation. Interestingly, the capacity for self-awareness and the ability to make and enjoy music are associated skills in the brain, which allow for emotional moments over time (Craig, 2015). Species (humans, certain birds, etc.) that create music are also able to recognize themselves in a mirror (Craig, 2015). This also involves expectation of satisfaction of what comes next musically (Craig, 2015). Even without any knowledge of music theory, one naturally feels auditory dissonance or incompletion of a chord progression or when a band is off tempo. When understanding consciousness, it is not one single mechanism which leads to the development of consciousness. Each aspect plays a part, like musicians in an orchestra, but it is only the sound of all players which results in the full product. Damasio (1999) elaborates that the self is the conductor, but the conductor was created by the orchestra. The internal sense of harmony for the self relies on these areas to play their part well.

Core gender is being constructed as a part of the proto-self. If we think of the proto-self as a big band, core gender is the bottom half of the rhythm section: percussion and bass. When those two are playing, you can tap your toe to it (if it's an uptempo or a ballad) but you would not know the song because the melody is not being played yet. This is the unarticulated but clearly felt sense of gender that a person feels without yet knowing. It is early mapping of the masculine and feminine aspects of the body without the language of masculine or feminine.

Damasio explains that the "Proto-self precedes basic feeling and both precede the feeling of knowing that constitutes core consciousness" (Damasio, 1999, p.281). Let's build onto the proto-self and work through how core consciousness brings with it the construction of the core self.

Core consciousness "is put in place by genome with a little help from the early environment" in humans (Damasio, 1999, p.200). Hameroff (2018) says life/consciousness began because of a feeling (on the cellular level); this feeling is likely a sense of reward for change which then led to more change. Core consciousness is defined by the sense of self in the present and, as stated previously, what precedes it is only a low-level awareness in the proto-self (Damasio, 1999). The birth of core consciousness involves the development of the organism's ability to process objects and put them into a context. It is from this primitive awareness that representation is created. It is not a language but one's inner sense that is based on images of feelings, as well as emotion. Consciousness emerges from a change in bodily states using a "universal nonverbal vocabulary of body signals. The apparent self emerges as the feeling of a feeling" (Damasio, 1999, p.31). Gendered interoception is emerging within these feelings of feelings.

Damasio (1999) explains that parts of the brain are "free to roam" (p.21) whereas other aspects are continuously mapping the body. Regulatory functions and body mapping do not create consciousness but are essential to the mechanisms from which core consciousness springs (Damasio, 1999). When brain mapping is in an equalized homeostatic range it is experienced as pleasing and is regulated by hormones and neuromodulators. Gender congruence/incongruence are foundational feelings which contribute to a balance within a person. The homeostatic nuclei are what create the "feeling of knowing" within the core self (Damasio, 2010, p.193). Feelings are the "barometer" of our state of being (Damasio, 2010, p.56). And as part of that state, gender emerges with the development of consciousness.

In tandem with core consciousness is the core self which is "about personhood but not necessarily identity" (Damasio, 2010, p.168). A sequence of images (representations of feelings, thoughts, objects in the mind) begin to create a narrative and a momentary pattern (Damasio, 2010). The core self is developed out of the proto-self's interaction with some object outside the body; the result of this encounter creates the core self (Damasio, 2010). The core self represents the individual in relation to the outside world and how this self is constructed from that impact. These early events of feeling an(other) or an object as differentiated from the self (going from a primordial feeling to a feeling of an(other)) are analogous to the developmental tasks in infancy to be discussed later, the child's ability to differentiate the self from another. Attention can now be directed towards an(other) thing. The act of perceiving an object elicits an emotional reaction that changes the primordial feeling which, in turn, alters the interoceptive map (Damasio, 2010). This is a present tense version of the self.

There is not a simple way to separate core consciousness and background feelings; they are intrinsically linked (Damasio, 1999). Through the complexity of interoceptive sensations, gender is tightly wrapped in core consciousness and is thus continuously running in the background out of conscious awareness. The burgeoning understanding and articulation of one's gender identity is formed through interactional experience with others. The interpretation of these background feelings of gender is being shaped by the interaction with the world. As will be explored in Chapter 3, the mirroring (primary infant/caregiver interactions) which occurs influences how the child understands and expresses their gendered feelings, along with other cultural forces of what it means to express masculinity and femininity.

The entirety of conscious thought and what can be known springs from core consciousness (Damasio, 1999). From core consciousness comes the core self which is continuously creating itself in response to every stimulus and includes all of our background emotions. Core consciousness is responsible for translating all our visceral feelings (which are resistant to language) into an I or me (Damasio, 1999). The "me"-ness of gender is not so easily translated into language, as was shown in Chapter 1, particularly since much of it is non-conscious. Understanding gender as a developing aspect of the proto-self and core self is supported by the primordial, unclassifiable nature of these sensations that resist language.

Autobiographical self

At the height of this topographical model of the self is the autobiographical self. It develops from the core self's ability to represent multiple objects throughout time. The autobiographical self has a recorded past and anticipated future of core self pulses (Damasio, 2010). According to Damasio (1999), body representations happen from the brainstem up to the cerebral cortex. The brainstem contributes to core consciousness whereas cortex contributions are necessary for extended consciousness, which is the type of consciousness necessary for an autobiographical self and the consciousness we generally exist in.

Autobiographical self and consciousness are about both personhood and identity (Damasio, 2010). This is when feelings of gender and the language of identity begin to converge. Edelman (2004) theorizes that the experience of qualia demonstrates the ability to make higher-order discriminations which are possible because of neural activity in the dynamic core, largely based in the thalamocortical system. Qualia are not a causal activity of consciousness but "a simultaneous property of that activity" (Edelman, 2004, p.78). Edelman (2004) refers to this fundamental consciousness as primary consciousness which then leads to higher-order consciousness where a self-concept with past and future is possible. The neural systems implicated in memory of the self and imagining a future fairly overlap with each other (Fernyhough, 2012).

In the autobiographical self, gender identity and expression take the shape we are accustomed to working with as clinicians. It has a past, present and future embodiment unless one has felt some incongruence impeding one's sense of self. It may feel impossible to imagine a future self if the past and present one is not fully understood or even felt depending on one's level of dissociation, dislocation or derealization. It may also be difficult to feel connected to one's past: "The most permanent thought and feeling in me almost all of my life was this feeling of just going through the motions" (Charl, quoted in Morgan, Marais & Wellbeloved, 2009, p.27). Charl is a South African trans man describing his sense of being prior to transition. In my clinical experience, I have observed many trans people (prior to transition) describe difficulties with imagining a future self or remembering their past. We will return to this concept further in Chapter 6 when we will examine time and trauma.

Genome establishes extended consciousness and is influenced by culture as well (Damasio, 1999). Extended consciousness is highly complex with multiple levels of organization. It continues to develop throughout the lifespan. Identity and sense of self are more advanced and multifaceted (Damasio, 1999). Creativity, reasoning, planning, etc. occur here but are supported by core consciousness. Extended consciousness develops the autobiographical self which is built from memories (Damasio, 1999). These memories and associations attach to our feelings about specifics of gendered existence through all our interpersonal (including culture) and intrapsychic experiences. The elements of gender expression are placed here in the autobiographical self since most of them are culturally contextual. The interplay of these elements will be expounded on in Chapter 4.

These three developments of self which lead to consciousness occur in separate but coordinated areas of the brain (Damasio, 2010). These percepts and images are located in the convergence-divergence regions of the brain. Convergence-divergence zones (CDZs) are microscopic collections of neurons in what are called convergence-divergence regions of the cerebral cortex. These areas function as feedforward-feedback loops of sensory information to and from the body (Damasio, 2010). In practical terms, the CDZs are about synchronization. A useful analogy is when we used to edit on film; picture and sound were on different reels. If the reels were not aligned using the clapboard mark, watching the dialogue would be disconcerting because the lip movement would not synch with the dialogue. Our visual and auditory cortical CDZs would be out of sync, producing uncomfortable emotions. It is actually more annoying when it is only subtly out of sync, whereas when it is obviously out of sync it usually produces laughter (like in the movie *Singing in the Rain*). What are the implications of this for gender incongruence? The CDZs may be the localized points for the desynchronization of gender one feels with gender dysphoria. The profound feelings of discrepancy in gender that trans people experience are not just a "belief" but concrete feelings permeating the mind and body, as the result of free energy.

Core gender is emergent with consciousness which leads to the development of the self. It is founded on non-conscious neural patterns representing the body in "pulses" (Damasio, 1999, p.176). The feelings of gender are some of those pulses. These "body loops" are how the individual perceives their body states through neural and humoral (chemicals in the bloodstream) signals. The body landscape is represented and changed on every level in the brain (Damasio, 1999). Our bodies and minds are engaged in a continuous reciprocal process. We can think of the self as consisting of this multilayer of interoceptive and other signals which the brain is updating and interpreting (Ainsley *et al.*, 2014; Apps & Tsakiris, 2014; Seth, 2013). Therefore, gender emerges and relates to these layers.

This establishes *where* we feel gender in our bodies. There is something gendered in most areas of the brain/body. My theory that gender is located in consciousness is initially founded on the fact that gender is a feeling or rather, more accurately, gender is feelings. It is also a fact that "consciousness and emotion are not separable" as consciousness begins as a feeling, and what gender feels like is the collection of non-verbal signals of the body (Damasio, 1999, p.16). One's gender identity is understood through and with these signals and the feeling within one's mind about those signals. The foundations for gender identity are formed in concert with consciousness.

Only the individual can know their consciousness and their gender. They are subjective and inseparable from each other. Just as I cannot know what someone else's consciousness is, neither can I know what their gender feels like to them. Qualia, according to Damasio (2010), are the accompanying musical score of the rest of our mental processes. Gender has its own qualia: phenomenal features. If consciousness is made up of qualia, one's subjectivity of gender is a cluster of qualia within the qualia of consciousness.

Gender expressions are the statements and execution of one's gender identity: what we recognize as masculine, feminine, androgynous and genderqueer, and how we feel about them. Our associations to all the cultural elements of gender help us decide how we want to perform our gender. And without consciousness, there would be no culture (Damasio, 2010).

Brain injury

What supports my theory that gender is intrinsically a part of consciousness and not just an aspect of personality or genitals? After profound brain injury, core gender and gender identity remain stable whereas aspects of personality can be affected. Damasio (2010) hypothesizes that an operational proto-self is possible even if cortical areas are damaged. Stroke can affect the autobiographical self; individuals can "forget" that their left side is paralyzed with right cerebral hemisphere damage (Damasio, 2010). There is also asomatognosia where patients temporarily cannot feel musculoskeletal perceptions even though they have a full sense of self and visceral access (Damasio, 2010). Even damage to the insula, which can disrupt body awareness and emotional awareness, does not produce a change in gender (Ibañez, Gleichgerrcht & Manes, 2010).

There is no documented evidence (I thoroughly searched Medline and other databases) of a brain injury causing change in gender identity. Even if most other aspects of the person's personality are affected, their core gender identity is not affected. Their gender expression may change, which supports my argument that gender expression is part of the autobiographical self in extended and higher-order consciousness. Even in the case of amnesia and profound loss of memory of who one is, gender identity is not lost.

Second, "impairments in extended consciousness are compatible with preserved core consciousness" (Damasio, 1999, p.201). This supports my idea that in the myriad impairments that can change personality in brain injury, core gender identity is not affected. "Bilateral damage to the prefrontal cortices, even if extensive, should not alter core consciousness" (Damasio, 1999, p.236).

The only article found related to brain injury and gender identity was a single case report from 2015 in *Australasian Psychiatry* titled "Gender dysphoria 'cured' by status epilepticus" (Parkinson, 2015). Given this case is the only one in the literature, it needs to be addressed. Parkinson's approach to this patient is clearly from a medical model frame, given the psychiatric jargon he uses to describe this person. Additionally, he does not cite the most current clinical literature on working with transgender people; he cites much older, objectifying, pathologizing research. He also switches back and forth on which pronoun he uses to refer to the patient. Since there is no notation indicating the patient's preferred pronoun, I will use male pronouns to reflect his current affirmed gender according to the report.

Parkinson's report describes a case of someone assigned male at birth who experienced a lifelong (since four years old) female gender identity. This patient, diagnosed with

Borderline Personality Disorder, suffered with poor affect regulation and substance abuse.

The patient was living as a woman ("convincingly" as Parkinson puts it (p.166); this is disconcerting since who has the right to decide on what makes a convincing woman) and had been receiving feminizing hormones for over two years when Parkinson first saw him. The patient presented to Parkinson for treatment of depression and anxiety, as well as support letters for gender-affirming surgeries. Five years prior, the patient had fallen from the balcony of his parents' home and was subsequently admitted to the brain injury unit. The computed tomography (CT) scan reported cerebral and cortical atrophy and a hypodense area of the right frontal lobe. This fall was "probably" a suicide attempt, according to Parkinson, but it is unclear why Parkinson does not know for sure. Did the patient deny it was an attempt or had they not even discussed it? The patient had reported gender dysphoria since age four, but prior to the fall was still living as male. After the fall, the patient continued the feminine gender-affirming path.

During this time, Parkinson describes the patient experiencing "vilification on a daily basis" by the teenagers in his housing project and that he was obsessively checking his appearance. It does not seem so obsessive to me to check one's appearance when you are being harassed daily about your gender. The patient was using drugs and alcohol to manage the anxiety and emotional distress. Parkinson characterizes this as "typical of the Borderline" (p.167). Another clinical approach could be that this patient was experiencing a high degree of harassment and minority stress without much support. Parkinson also includes petty larceny and shoplifting as part of the Borderline diagnosis, which may be attributed to poverty and addiction. The patient eventually becomes homeless.

Soon after, the patient experienced a status epilepticus[1] which lasted about 45 minutes and required admission to the emergency department and then to the brain injury unit again. His CT scan and EEG showed no differences from those seven years prior, indicating no further damage. The patient at that time began reporting "misgivings" about the gender transition (p.167). Rather quickly, the patient asked to be called his prior male name and affirmed a male identity. By this time, he was homeless and had spent his inheritance on breast augmentation surgery. Parkinson reports that a "delighted mother came to the rescue" offering the money for reversal breast surgery (p.167). The patient began hormonal treatment to reactivate his endogenous testosterone production. He went to live with the mother and remained socially isolated.

Parkinson reveals something very important in his statement about the mother and her delight in reversing feminine gender attributes. The mother was obviously *not* delighted about the feminine gender of her adult child and felt no need to "rescue" him when he was living as female and experiencing constant harassment and homelessness. I do not believe that we can take this case as one of gender dysphoria being "cured" by an epileptic seizure. The external circumstances point to a person who experienced a tremendous amount of discrimination and minority stress when he transitioned; he had co-occurring mental health issues and may have had familial pressure to live as male in order to gain emotional and financial support.

In consideration of the original brain injury from the fall from the balcony, the patient's feminine identity remained intact. The brain scan remained unchanged

---

1   "A single prolonged seizure or a series of seizures without intervening full recovery of consciousness" (Merriam-Webster, 2017).

even when he decided to live as male. It seems that the "change" could have been an effect of the social milieu or some other reason, but I do not think we can say it is because of the brain injury. The epileptic seizure seems like the last of a string of traumatic events exacerbated by poverty, transphobia, poor affect regulation skills and familial rejection. The patient may have felt unable to go on unsupported living as a trans woman. Of course, we cannot know exactly what happened with this person, who needed more help than he received and who does not seem to have been consulted or collaborated with on this case study. Parkinson presumes to know without asking the subject.

Gender and humanity

Animal feelings are vaguer and simpler (Craig, 2015). Even though animals have a primary consciousness, they cannot consider concepts of past and future, which are necessary features of higher-order consciousness in the capability to develop a concept of self (Edelman, 2004). Lower-level consciousness is a feature of our brains that provides us with the present moment and is a level of consciousness that animals experience (Searles, 1997). It does not contain the element of the being having the capacity to reflect on itself: self-consciousness. This is present in higher-order consciousness, which is signaled by the presence of language (Edelman, 1989). Self-consciousness is the necessary element required for complex, nuanced gender identity and expression; this is not present in non-humans.

This may be an arrow pointing towards gender developing with higher-order consciousness and a fundamental difference between humans and animals. Transgender is not present in animals (as far as we know), which may be because they do not experience feelings in their bodies in the same manner that humans do. Subjectivity, being a human experience, leads one to think about how one feels and have ideas (and ultimately language) about it. Higher-order consciousness enables one to experience more complex feelings of self, such as feeling one's gender, which produces certain emotions. These emotions can be for most trans people dysphoric.

Self-reflexive gender is an aspect of human experience. It is comparable to the feeling of humanness. This sense of being is so profoundly meaningful that when it is disconfirmed by the body it becomes an intolerable feeling. I believe this is one way we can understand why the suicidal ideation rates are so high in the trans community. The high rates of suicidal ideation and attempts in TGNC people are at a clinical crisis. The National Transgender Discrimination Survey conducted in the U.S.A. and analyzed by the Williams Institute and the American Foundation for Suicide Prevention found startling numbers: 46 percent of trans men and 42 percent of trans women reported having attempted suicide, nine times the general population (Haas, Rodgers & Herman, 2014). These numbers are even higher when one factors in those who are disclosing (not stealth) their transgender status. Suicidal ideation rates across the lifespan can be as high as 96.5 percent (Adams, Hitomi & Moody, 2017). I do not think minority stress alone accounts for such a high disparity in suicidality in comparison with other minority groups. If the reader could imagine that they were to live each day with their bodies and environment disconfirming their humanity, they may be able to empathize. The constant implicit and explicit wearing down of one's sense of self and humanness through bodily dissonance, social misgendering and misrecognition could deteriorate one's capacity to live.

The purpose of these first two chapters has been to locate the reader in a theory of gender which is grounded in interoceptive and exteroceptive interplay through the FEP and inhabiting various levels of consciousness from core gender in the proto-self through full gender identity and expression in the autobiographical self. The next chapter will examine the early interpersonal experience of being trans through the lenses of developmental and clinical psychology.

CHAPTER 3

Mirroring Recognition

The being and knowing of the self as a private, embodied, subjective experience was established in the previous chapters. This chapter builds on this internalist theory to develop the externalist theory of the gendered self as one interacts with others and how that shapes personality and gender expression. It will continue to explore shame, particularly related to transphobia, and how we work through this phenomenon in psychotherapy and explore how "the struggle for recognition is the struggle for existence itself" (Rochat, 2009, p.203).

The following will examine the developmental trajectory of trans and gender diverse children. By this I mean multiple groups of individuals: those who transitioned in adulthood and did not "know" they were trans as children; those kids who are able to verbally articulate their transgender identity and adults and children who were/are gender nonconforming but do not identify as trans. I want to acknowledge that there are people who feel comfortable in their assigned gender and later on, in adulthood, do not. This chapter does not propose to speak about their experience, since they likely felt that the mirroring they received was attuned to their gender at the time.

This is an interactional, interpersonal developmental theory of being gender diverse and not identifying with the sex assigned at birth. This will be done through interrogating how mirroring affects perception security, attachment and shame. Furthermore, it will explore the consequences of the ways in which the mirroring of gender complicates these states for the individual. By mirroring I mean to include the active and tacit verbal and embodied attunement of caregivers to the child.

Development

Before we begin to talk about gender, let us quickly establish the developmental milestones and trajectory of an emergence of a self in children. Primary intersubjectivity, the ability of the infant to engage with another, emerges at six weeks old when the infant develops the ability to smile in actual response to social interaction and can thus engage in dyadic communication (Rochat, 2009; Trevarthen, 1979). By two months, infants are able to have reciprocal exchanges with others—conversations without language (Bigelow & Rochat, 2006). From three to five months old infants demonstrate some proprioceptive-visual synchrony discernment (Rochat & Morgan, 1995). The baby sees a behavior, such as sticking out your tongue, and can imitate that behavior. It has also been found that viseo-tactile precedes viseo-proprioceptive integration as it relates to the feeling of having a body (Cowie, Makin & Bremner, 2013). This signals the beginning skills for self–other differentiation and the infant having a sense of its own body. At seven months, disapproval–approval mirroring cues are responded to by the infant (Kleeman, 1971). That infants can discern and react to positive and negative mirroring will be key to the points made in this chapter. In the period between seven and nine months, infants employ gesture to communicate and influence another person (Rochat, 2009). By eight months, separation anxieties emerge (Rochat, 2009). The child can feel the caregiver's absence. Secondary intersubjectivity arises as the nine-month-old has the ability to relate to objects with shared attention with another person (Rochat, 2009). The infant is aware of and keeps checking on the other's attention to the object. At one year the child's gender in the parent's mind is already established (Kleeman, 1971). This is not to say that the parents are not projecting their gender expectations on the child before then. Then by 14 months, a child will begin to copy another person's actions, even if those actions are not efficient, which demonstrates the child is able to take the other's perspective (Rochat, 2009). By 18–20 months the infant can recognize him/herself in the mirror (Craig, 2015; Gallup, Anderson & Platek, 2011; Rochat, 2009). Interestingly, the anterior insular cortex is implicated in self-recognition in the mirror test (Devue *et al.*, 2007).

Then by two to three years old, children are thinking about others in decisions about their own behavior and actions as well as registering embarrassment (Rochat, 2009). This is also when the child can begin to label their own gender, and by three to six years old gender is a stable trait and the child can self-label their gender (Kohlberg, 1966; Thompson, 1975). I would like to note here that gender self-labeling is well-established, which reinforces that it is possible that trans children can know their gender by this point in their development as well. The temporality of self also takes shape by about age three (Rochat, 2009). These developmental milestones demonstrate the progression of bodily ownership, the development of a gendered subjective self and the interactional importance of others in this process.

Mirror stage

The development of self is intrinsically linked with the mirror stage (Lacan, 1977; Pines, 1985; Winnicott, 1971). Every child acquires "imaginary mastery" over the image of the body through Lacan's mirror stage. The infant takes in their image through the aid of the primary Other, naming the infant in the mirror. Thus, the foundation for the development of the "I" (the ego) through the real mirror and with interactions with the primary caregiver is set (Lacan, 1977). The ego is foundationally a body ego, a projection from the surface of the body, similar to the cortical homunculus (Freud, 1923). What Freud was missing was the internal milieu. My theory also takes a different spin on the phrase "anatomy is destiny" (1923, p.178) spun by Freud to demonstrate the power of the phallus. It all depends on which aspects of our anatomy (brain over genitals) we listen to as to what the shape is of that destiny.

The first mirror is the primary caregiver's face (Kleeman, 1971). Mirroring is not only identification of the self in the mirror but includes how the infant is held, spoken to, played with, comforted by the primary caregiver (Winnicott, 1971). The caregiver's ability to be a "good enough mirror" by responding to the child's individual needs will provide the child with a sense of "basic trust" (Winnicott, 1971; Erikson, 1963). Erikson deliberately said individual needs in order to emphasize attunement *to that specific child*, to facilitate a "sense of being 'all right', of being oneself" (Erikson, 1963, p.249). The gap between "good-enough" and perfect is bridged within the child's mental life (Winnicott, 1971). It is the child's mentalization which releases the caregiver from being perfect.

The self is not only a private construct but one that is outside the self in the space between people (Rochat, 2009). Rochat (2009) also explains that mirror recognition is linked to the sense of normative self-representation: How do I compare to others? He proves this through two experiments he conducted with small children. In the first experiment, a mark was placed on the children's foreheads without their knowledge and the children quickly removed the mark when they saw themselves in the mirror. In the opposite experiment, everyone in the room had the same mark and the children did not remove it when they noticed it in their reflection. "Social conformity modulates their expression of self-consciousness" (Rochat, 2009, p.217).

During the mirror stage, the child develops the understanding that "I am separate from the other." A sort of "detachment of the self from himself takes place, which is the initiation of an alienation" (Frølund, 1997, p.43). One could say, I am alienated from myself in that I can think about and observe myself. I am my self and I can think about my self. For some trans and gender nonconforming (TGNC) children, this sense that "I am a separate person" begins to transform into alienation from my own sense of my internal perceptions (interoceptive awareness) and I begin to trust others' perceptions of me more than my own. The person develops what we understood in the first chapter as "misinteroception" (Paulus & Stein, 2010). The alienation occurs through the primary others disconfirming the child's gendered self, whereas on the contrary, reliable interoceptive awareness can protect against self–other boundary fuzziness (Fotopoulou & Tsakiris, 2017).

Mirroring contributes to the construction of perceiving and identifying one's internal cues. Interoception develops early and is believed to be a relatively stable constitutional trait (Garfinkel *et al.*, 2015). Mallorquí-Bagué and colleagues (2016) think of interoception as a trait similar to temperament, a baseline aspect of one's self. A study by

Weisz, Balázs & Ádám (1988) reinforces the relationship between mirroring and self-attunement when conducting the heart beat detection experiment mentioned earlier which correlates with higher interoceptive sensitivity. They found when subjects looked in the mirror during the test, their accuracy (IAcc) improved significantly. The mirroring of the self may make it more of an emotional (pleasant) experience. This led Ádám to hypothesize that visceroception and emotion are an "interwoven phenomenon" which mutually affect each other (Ádám, 1998, p.115).

The Weisz study explicates how the mirror (real and symbolic) aids in locating the self within the body for the subject. It upends the judgment of transgender people who are perceived as looking at themselves in the mirror too much. It is not narcissism (for most people, of course—there are narcissistic trans people, just as there are in every other group of people) but a means of developing a better connection with the self. It is trying to locate oneself in that mirror, particularly during bodily changes; one needs the mirror to mentalize and incorporate how one looks now. Fotopoulou & Tsakiris (2017) state that our "physical body itself is not passively perceived but actively mentalized" (p.10). Fotopoulou and Tsakiris' example is that in seeing one's body in the mirror we have a unified experience of that perception; it is a whole, built on the integration of multisensory information from all regions within the body.

IAcc was also found to correlate with eye contact. Those people who had good eye contact were better able to rate their subjective emotions in connection to interoceptive signals (Baltazar *et al.*, 2014). A crucial aspect of mirroring and feeling in tune with another is one's ability to maintain eye contact. Given the higher rates of autism spectrum disorder in the trans community, this places many of them at a deficit in relation to registering their feelings.

These examples reinforce how we are not subjects alone but always intersubjectively connected. Working from this interactional model of how the core self begins to be shaped by others, I want to draw on Fotopoulou & Tsakiris' (2017) work which puts forward that the burgeoning self is created as an embodied interactional dance with primary caregivers. They make the connection between an infant's ability to understand their interoceptive identification and the child's subjective embodied interaction with primary caretakers. These interoceptive identifications are some of the foundational substances of the self. The caregiver's ability to mentalize the child's mental state provides the ability to congruently mirror for the child. Parental embodied mentalization (PEM) reflects the parents' ability to mirror kinesthetically and intuit the child's mental state, offering it back to the infant; then the multisensory signals can be integrated into predictive models according to the free energy principle (Fotopoulou & Tsakiris, 2017; Shai & Belsky, 2011). This also implies that the parent can modify their own embodiment to accommodate for the child. Fotopoulou & Tsakiris (2017) further define it as "the on-going, dynamic process of maintaining and updating generative models of likely causes of sensory data from inside the body itself and the external world" (p.10). This sensory data is in multisensory bundles between bodies hopefully attuned and working towards integration. In the infant's early life, the majority of their interactions are not coordinated, but the key to positive PEM is the parent's ability to manipulate their kinesthetics to respond to the child. It is not about getting it right the first time but one's ability to adjust accordingly. This attunement provides the child with an embodied sense of self in relation to others (Shai & Belsky, 2011). In the case of TGNC children, their multisensory experience of their gender will likely not be understood or integrated for them by a caregiver. The result of low PEM experiences is that a child's mental states are "ignored, distorted or overridden" and the child will not understand or trust their embodiment (Shai & Belsky, 2011, p.178). This is what is at stake for TGNC children. Their predictive models begin to develop from low PEM which skews their priors in relation to their sensory experience.

The infant's ability to integrate all this sensory input in time and space, this embodied process, is building the foundation of the self. This is intrinsically linked with the caregiver's body as it is meshed with the infant's in early life in order to take care of the infant's basic needs (Fotopoulou & Tsakiris, 2017). Fotopoulou & Tsakiris (2017) argue that even with a poorly mentally responding caregiver, there will be some embodied attunement for a minimal self to take shape. Conceived as proximal embodied interactions, they propose that the foundational feelings of self begin in social interactions. But what if the social milieu is indifferent or rejecting of how you comport your body? The child is not given the clues to understand their own body. Good-enough caregiving is not only mental attunement but foundationally embodied through our bodies in the figurative and literal holding environment like Harlow's soft monkeys (Fotopoulou & Tsakiris, 2017).

It is not just that social mentalization aids in constituting the self; another main purpose of infant/caregiver interaction is the achievement of homeostasis since the infant cannot produce actions to regulate their body and environment. It allows the child to eventually mentalize their own homeostasis (Fotopoulou & Tsakiris, 2017). This reinforces the argument made in the preceding chapters that self-awareness is foundationally from the body. Fotopoulou & Tsakiris (2017) reinforce that paradoxically embodied mentalization is a process between bodies, not minds. If we can recognize that the absence of good-enough

PEM is a developmental trauma, then misgendered PEM must be equally recognized.

(Mis)Gendering mirrors

No one looks in the mirror at their genitals to recognize themselves. They look at their face, just as everyone else looks at their face. How one's gender is read determines how she will be engaged with by others. Observation and research show how adults interact along gendered lines with infants such as by playing more roughly with boys and cuddling a girl, or that girls are talked to more than boys (Brooks-Gunn & Matthews, 1979). Additionally, in one seminal study, adults attributed different feelings to nine-month-old infants based on what gender the infant was labeled by researchers: crying was identified as fear for "girls" and anger for "boys" (Condry & Condry, 1976). One can see how the adult's projection onto the child would influence how they would then provide comfort, which may or may not match what the child actually needs from them. In another study, mothers were found to touch infants assigned male at birth, as opposed to being more vocal with female-assigned infants (Lewis, 1972).

The infamous Baby X experiment demonstrated not only the effect based on the perceived gender of the three-month-old infant, but that there was an effect based on the gender of the adult. If the child was identified as a girl by researchers, male and female participants used more gender-stereotypical toys. In the cases of unknown gender, men handled the children less and chose the most neutral toys, making "safer" choices (according to the researchers) while women physically handled the infants more (Seavey, Katz & Rosenberg Zalk, 1975). They concluded that the gender of the adult and the gender assigned to the baby affected what toys were offered the child. It was also interesting to note that when no gender was assigned to the infant, the adults "found" evidence for their guesses; such as a strong grip if they guessed boy or soft features for a girl. The researchers also described the "no-gender" part of the experiment as stressful for the adults. Adults were uncomfortable with not knowing the gender of the baby. This is not particularly surprising given our cultural imperative to first ask what gender a baby is before even asking about its health or the historical practice of operating on intersex infants' genitals to conform to "norms" even though in most cases there was no physical medical reason to do so (Intersex Society of North America, 2006).

It has been found that parents who share the same gender as the assigned gender at birth for the child were the caregivers with the most distress about a child's gender nonconformity (Burnes *et al.*, 2016). Burnes and colleagues' interviews with trans adults showed that the distress of the parent took the form of bullying, verbal abuse and coercion to deny TGNC identity from childhood through adulthood. D'Augelli, Grossman and Starks (2006) found that gender nonconforming youth have higher rates of victimization (verbal, physical and sexual abuse), as compared to their lesbian, gay or bisexual gender conforming peers.

Parents have an "illusion" of what is expected from a boy or girl and interact with their children accordingly in implicit and explicit ways (Kleeman, 1971). The power of parental projection is no stranger to clinicians. We are almost always working towards unmooring parental projection that patients have introjected.

"Good-enough" mirroring is a foundational need of all children and has lifelong implications. The branches of effect are to one's sex life, self-regulation, emotional regulation, interpersonal relationships and ability to parent (Gergely & Watson, 1996; Mikulincer and Shaver, 2007; Scharff, 1982). Without appropriate mirroring, the child's "own creative capacity begins to atrophy" (Winnicott, 1971, p.2). Every child's survival depends upon being seen. The TGNC child follows the other's gaze, but their sense of themselves is usually not reflected back, as many of our clinical experiences have shown. Mis-attuned mirroring affects the child's interoceptive sensitivity and accuracy. For TGNC children, their body is already complicated and may be on the road to dissociation. If the child's body-image is developed from incongruently gendered mirroring, it scrapes against their body-schema. It amplifies the prediction error and skews their felt body matrix.

Good-enough mirroring enables the infant to develop more accuracy in their interoceptive inferences, which then leads to better interoceptive awareness (Fotopoulou & Tsakiris, 2017). This is predictive of emotional self-regulation and thus its absence puts the child at risk for emotional disorders (Garfinkel *et al.*, 2015). As can be seen through the interoceptive research, when the infant is not attuned to and mentalized by an appropriately embodied parent, a "developmental cascade" can occur with the body matrix since the child begins to ignore their own bodily signals due to the disruption of external factors, which makes them believe the internal signals are untrustworthy (Badoud & Tsakiris, 2017; Shai & Belsky 2011). The psyche's choice then becomes to deny the self (the gender hyperprior) in order to conserve energy. The dysregulated human as it relates to gender is exhausting. The child, at a certain point, gives in, unconsciously and/or consciously and assumes that his/her/their sense of their body is wrong.

The TGNC child has their own exceptional experience of mis-attunement. Gender is even more complicated and deeper than other experiences of poor attunement, reaching into who we are as a conscious being, our core self.

The Winnicottian false self develops as a product of the child's effort to conform to the gender assigned at birth, to fill in that space between what the caregiver can offer and what the child actually needs (Winnicott, 1965).[1] The child assigned male at birth who experiences herself as feminine but who is mirrored maleness submits to the false "maleness" as a matter of survival. The other's needs and perceptions override the child's own sense of self and a dissociative defensive style becomes entrenched. This tension is exacerbated into an unbearable rub when gender incongruence is part of the constellation of experiences. Children quickly learn that their gender in private is at odds with the world, consciously and unconsciously. This is a subliminal and unarticulated process for most TGNC children. These children begin to consciously or unconsciously manipulate their behavior away from their body-matrix (ignoring their interoceptive perceptions) and to a body-image (and expression) that matches others' expectations. For all people there is "basic dissonance" between the public and private view of the self (Rochat, 2009, p.27). Rochat explains that the me I have in my mind is always a compilation of these first and third person perspectives and that others contribute foundationally to self-consciousness. However, for TGNC children it is on a more profound level.

Attachment

We have evolved to avoid social rejection (Rochat, 2009). It is in our physical and psychological interest. This is exemplified by the universal feeling of separation anxiety and development of attachment styles. Attachment styles

---

1   See Langer (2016) for my critique of Lemma's interpretation of mirroring and transgender women.

are related to infants' responses to internal and external stressors (Hill-Soderlund *et al.*, 2008). Attachment styles are thought to create internal working models (IWMs) from which the individual is predicting the likely outcome of certain attachment behaviors and expectation of care from others. Our attachment styles remain relatively stable through adulthood and set the stage for how we handle interpersonal relationships (Mikulincer and Shaver, 2007). We know TGNC children experience harassment and rejection by immediate family which affects their internal working models (Gordon & Meyer, 2007; Grossman *et al.*, 2005). These IWMs have far-reaching effects and place children at risk for all subtypes of insecure attachment. Two studies looked at how attachment style affected the processing of emotionally salient facial expressions of strangers. Their results indicated that those with insecure attachment styles could detect changes in emotion faster than other styles (Frayley *et al.*, 2006; Niedenthal *et al.*, 2002). It has also been found that those with anxious attachment are more apt to respond to negative cues, whereas avoidant style adults are more dismissive of positive cues (Rognoni *et al.*, 2008). The negative self-construction developed out of these IWMs creates a perception of others as unavailable and that I am not worthy of help. These are compounded when we include the reality of transphobia.

A 2010 study of attachment styles by Vitelli and Riccardi found that trans participants (who were already engaged in medical transition) had insecure attachment 72.25 percent higher than their controls. This was a small (n=18) clinical sample, not a general population sample, which biases it towards insecure attachment styles. Interestingly, they used the MMPI as part of their assessment and found no co-occurring psychopathology, not unlike Keo-Meier and colleagues (2014).

As Vitelli and Riccardi (2010) found, insecure attachment, in general, can be related to traumas in the family or in adulthood, such as childhood physical abuse and loss of an early attachment figure; this was particularly the case for the trans women in the study. Their hypothesis was that one's transness is the symptom of the poor attachment and/or trauma, which is like Fonagy's (1997) arguments. Most professionals actually working in trans health do not subscribe to this formulation since, as one person joked to me, if everyone who had poor mirroring and attachment was trans, there would be a lot more trans people in the world.

A 2017 study found higher levels of separation anxiety disorder in children assigned male at birth (AMAB) referred to gender clinics (VanderLaan *et al.*, 2017). They concluded that this finding was part of a larger pattern of internalizing problems by these children. When one's gendered self is unrecognizable or pathologized, it is a likely consequence that one will turn to internalizing as a defense. This may be due to insecure attachment, but we should also have in mind that it is scary to meet new people when you feel insecure in your gender as well. In an interview for the book *Trans Voices*, Leo recounts how he felt as a child: "Going to unknown places and meeting unfamiliar people was too traumatic for me. All I wanted to do was stay at home where I felt safe and comfortable" (Henry, 2017, p.20).

What I have been trying to show at this juncture is that the inadequate mirroring and related insecure attachment could be a result of rejection of gender nonconformity or it could be exacerbated by it. Through my clinical lens, there are two hypotheses from which to work. The first hypothesis is that poor attachment is due to the child's gender transgression which triggers parental rejection for crossing gender norms. This results in parent/child interactions with tacit or explicit coercion to gender norms. We know that trans individuals experience more harassment, discrimination and violence compared to their siblings (Factor & Rothblum, 2007). Furthermore, poor mirroring/attachment may have already been present due to the myriad reasons (maternal depression, intergenerational trauma, unresolved pathological family dynamics, etc.) and may be worsened due to gender transgressions. Both of these are more probable in relation to trans women since femininity in AMAB children is policed more than masculinity in assigned female at birth (AFAB) children.

The second hypothesis is that poor attachment is due to the internal gender trauma (more prediction error, increased free energy) that TGNC children could be experiencing because of not being able to live in their experienced gender. This may interfere with their ability to connect to others, due to their own alienation from their bodies and having to act in an incongruent gender role. Many patients have been socially awkward or described as odd by other people, since they feel so uncomfortable trying to make a life in the gender assigned at birth. This is supported from my practice by the experiences of individuals who express how much easier it feels to interact with others post-transition, since they are more comfortable with themselves and their role. Of course, this is only one layer of interpersonal emotional intelligence and does not suddenly make everyone an extrovert. Many people need to work through building up other interpersonal skills and overcoming a history of being bullied or ostracized. It is much easier to do this though once free energy is reduced and they are not battling so much internal noise.

Interoceptive perception can be affected by an individual's attachment style. Affective touch and pain at the skin level are considered a subcategory of interoception even though the individual is technically perceiving on the outside of their body. This signaling provides homeostatic information that has two understandings: an affective quality (i.e. pleasant vs. painful) and a social meaning (i.e. care vs. harm). We believe that oxytocin is released in the brain when there is positive touch between primary caregivers and infants, as well as between adults (Uvnäs-Moberg, Handlin & Petersson, 2014). Therefore, insecure attachment styles could be associated with an oxytocin system which is deficient (Uvnäs-Moberg, Handlin & Petersson, 2014). In the study of older infants, we know that they can be soothed by others through affective touch or by self-soothing methods (Beebe & Lachmann, 1998; Rothbart, Ziaie & O' Boyle, 1992). Nine-month-olds have been found to positively physically react to affective touch (Fairhurst, Löken & Grossmann, 2014).

Affective touch also runs through a different afferent path than just skin mechanoreceptors. It relies on C-fibers (which only respond to slow touch (i.e. gentle caressing)) which take a pathway to the thalamus and then to the posterior insular cortex (the insula being implicated in interoception) (Craig, 2015; Morrison, Bjornsdotter & Olausson, 2011). Affective touch is at once internal and interpersonal, related to homeostatic regulation and social-emotional bonding. This is to reinforce the importance of interoception and affective touch, since in mirroring there has been a bias towards the visual, verbal and proprioceptive aspects of mirroring, and to highlight the importance of embodied mirroring (Fotopoulou & Tsakiris, 2017; Shai & Belsky, 2011). Affective touch is an action that comforts us; it is an essential emotional regulation tool.

Our predictive models of pain are related to our embodied social interactions when we were developing our attachment style (Fotopoulou & Tsakiris, 2017). Krahé and colleagues (2015) looked at how pain modulation is dependent on "embodied" social support and the attachment style which dictates how that social interaction is perceived by the individual. In their study, they found contrasting reactions to affective touch based on attachment style, which is similar to the finding of other researchers (Sambo *et al.*, 2010). Higher attachment anxiety was related to an increase in subjective pain, whereas high attachment avoidance found a decrease in pain. When social support was factored in, the inverse was found. Empathy plus touch reduced subjective pain for the attachment anxiety group and increased it for the avoidant, which makes sense because the avoidant style person prefers to cope alone. This is important because trans people who undergo electrolysis or surgical interventions will need to know how best to manage pain and find ways to appropriately comfort themselves. How best can we provide preparation, support and interventions in order to manage emotional and physical pain in order to help patients avoid dissociation?

I was talking with a patient who was in the hospital one day post-operation. He was in pain across multiple areas of his body and feeling quite scared and desperate. He reached out to me for help in this crisis. It was particularly unnerving for me since he is an extraordinarily positive and resilient person. These moments are the delicate balance between the therapist's position as arbiter of hope and reality. What could I offer? I hoped it would be OK for him but I did not know and I felt it would be remiss of me to offer blind optimism about the success of surgery. I first offered him what felt to me like some flailing efforts at support, hoping that my voice was enough of a container. Then something occurred to me. Sometimes I have images or thoughts that pop into my head in clinical moments. At this point in my career and understanding the principles of psychoanalysis, I understand these moments as the patient's unconscious communicating to my unconscious. In that moment on the phone, I had the image of rocking and soothing him. Of course, I would not do that, but I had just been reading the research on affective touch. So, I suggested to him that he ask his partner to stroke his arm (affective touch) to help soothe him (he was unable to be hugged or held due to the post-surgery restrictions). This intervention struck him well and in an emotional way. The reason, I think, this resonated with him (and on a more profound affective level) was because his pain and fear tapped into the primary failure of embodied mirroring by his primary caregivers (globally, not just related to gender) which may have left him as a baby unsoothed and left adrift. Given his history, this made sense to both of us. In that moment, he needed more than my symbolic mirroring and needed real embodied attunement.

Internalized transphobia: Shame by another name

Shame is the specter of many a psychotherapy. It is particularly acute during this time in our culture when trans visibility has been accompanied by increases in transphobic rhetoric, hate crimes, transphobic legislation proposals and attempted bans on transgender armed services members (sadly, this is just snapshot of what is happening in America). We do not practice in a bubble, nor does anyone transition in one. Even in the future, when there is more cultural acceptance, there will still be the personal and familial phobia of gender transgression in thought and action. With this in mind, let us focus on how mirroring and attachment factor into shame for TGNC people.

By three years old, a child can register shame, embarrassment, self-deprecation and humor (Rochat, 2009).

According to Lewis (1992) shame is a self-conscious emotion activated by a real or "imagined other." Zahavi (2014) argues that it cannot be thought of without the social context and our awareness of being seen by others. Consequently, shame suppresses self-esteem and magnifies one's sense of one's perceived or real shortcomings. Zahavi builds on Sartre, in that shame is both relational and personal.

Our evolutionary basic affiliation need (BAN) drives us to fear social ostracism, and the direct expression of that fear is shame (Rochat, 2009). Social affiliation is a basic need of psychical and physical survival. Rochat defines shame as "*the avoidant behavioral expression of being exposed to public scrutiny*" and is the sibling to humiliation (2009, p.113, italics in original). It is always connected to the other's gaze, either real or incorporated into our superego (Fuchs, 2003). Once it is introjected, no others are needed for the individual to perpetuate this judgment. Shame is an intersubjective process where the control feels as if it is in others, whereas guilt is about something I have done wrong (Rochat, 2009). Or put another way, when a negative social evaluation is internalized to a negative self-evaluation that becomes shame (Dickerson, Gruenewald & Kemeny, 2004).

Self-consciousness arises out of the profound fear of social rejection (Rochat, 2009). We co-construct our selves in interaction with others, which begins in mirroring (Rochat, 2009). Shame is being an object: that we have fallen from a subjective person to an "it" (Sartre, 1992). This non-human designation from others is a common fear among trans people. We are a failure of normality and barred from it (Zahavi, 2014). The exclusion from normality is at the core of objective and internalized transphobia. Trans people are institutionally excluded from normality by the absence of trans and non-binary genders as options on most forms one fills out in school, work and medical settings; there are only binary gendered restrooms in most spaces; they are not counted in the United States Census; and trans health is not being taught in medical training, to name a few examples. (This is also why when comparing trans people to other gendered people, we say "cisgendered" persons instead of "normal" people.) Tackling the institutional is not the focus for this book; let us zoom in on the intimate, implicit, relational aspects of this phenomenon.

Children receive pre-linguistic expression through embodied mentalization and mirroring which enables them to be socially visible; without recognition, one becomes invisible as a person (Honneth, 2001). This functions as an erasure of the self. How does this function for the TGNC person and relate to internalized transphobia?

Gesture is an unconscious act developed from the body matrix. The neural circuitry for gesture precedes verbal language (Ramachandran & Blakeslee, 1998). Gesture is usually the first public display of gender variance. As we know, parental rejection may be due to aversion to their child's gender nonconformity (Grossman *et al.*, 2005). TGNC people commonly remember when the disgust or disapproval crossed their parents' eyes when they transgressed some gender norm. Or it may have been more explicit: the child was humiliated by a parent who yelled at them to "stop walking like a girl." The following is a quote from a 21-year-old, white, trans man interviewed about his internalized transphobia:

> Generally, I have a lot of shame connected with that [my gender]. I guess it's my upbringing, and what I heard about transgender people growing up. I guess the shame must be from knowing and hearing all these negative things. (Rood *et al.*, 2017, p.9)

This study boiled down the messaging of shame into discrete themes through interviews with trans adults: it is shameful to identify as trans; shame blocks taking action towards affirming gender; there is shame at not meeting stereotypical gender norms; one should expect to be victimized (Rood *et al.*, 2017). What this research highlights for clinical work is that shame runs through the entire process of transition *and* living as one's affirmed gender over the rest of the lifespan. This quote is a trans woman's recollection of implicit shame related to her cross-gender behavior as a child:

> I instinctively knew that it was taboo to have dressed in my sister's underclothes. But there was a part of my brain that didn't want me to reveal myself because it protected me from the shame I would have felt if my father caught me. (Henry, 2017, p.76)

For some trans people no memory exists of that kind of particular moment, but the messaging of acceptable gender embodiment was communicated through the earliest of mirroring and embodied mentalization. In line with this idea, in the Rood and colleagues study interviews, many of the trans people interviewed either struggled or could not say where or when they learned the messages that their gender variance was wrong (Rood *et al.*, 2017). Pavlov demonstrated almost a hundred years ago the power of non-conscious, viscerosensory learned reflexes (1926). Gendered reflexive gestures can also be unlearned with the negative reinforcement of humiliation. As Poppy articulates in *Trans Voices*: "Even at a young age, I forced myself to snap out of it and tried to fit in [with gender norms]" (Henry, 2017, p.78). These aspects of gender are tacitly known. Polanyi (1966) demonstrates tacit knowledge by discussing experiments where people are given a shock when they see a certain syllable. The subjects begin to avoid those syllables, even though they could not answer consciously what those syllables were. This is analogous to the implicit shame transmitted to the child and the child altering their gesture and mental life accordingly.

This implicit phenomenon can trigger the core gender body-schema to foreclose and a false body-image and false self (the gender assigned at birth) to replace it. Winnicott (1971) described this phenomenon of inadequate mirroring in this way: "any minute the mother's face will become fixed or her mood will dominate, and my own personal needs must then be withdrawn otherwise my central self may suffer insult" (p.2). Muller (1985) captured the child's necessity to fulfill the other's need as such: "the mirror phase…establishes the framework for intersubjective illusion insofar as it enables the child now to mirror the mother's desire, to be what the mother wants so as to please her" (p.238).

Shame in small amounts can regulate omnipotent feelings, as well as regulating external stimuli through minor failures of the caregiver to respond as expected by the child. This helps the child see a difference between "I" and "other." If early shame dominates, it loses its regulatory function; defensiveness predominates, with dissociation, projective identification and splitting (Frølund, 1997). Frølund goes on to distinguish between what he calls mature shame in the neurotic who is introspective and self-reflective, and early shame, which impacts the individual's personality development more profoundly. The person's ability to relate is more fragile and is characterized in treatment differently. Whereas neurotics can speak their conflicts, the severely neurotic or psychotic structures act out their conflicts affectively in the therapeutic relationship. Frølund says:

> The child has an external experience of himself placed at two different places at the same time, both in his own perception of himself and in the mirror image of the mother, yet referring to one and the same person. Hereby, the tension between private and social self-awareness and between the subjective and the objective is established. (Frølund, 1997, p.43)

One of the costs for suppressing the self is shame. This tacit shame infiltrates the body and begins the war within it. We know that internalized transphobia is associated with mental health issues, suicidality and poorer self-concept (Breslow *et al.*, 2015; Perez-Brumer *et al.*, 2015; Reyes *et al.*, 2016; Testa *et al.*, 2015). This quote from a multiracial, 26-year-old trans man captures this:

> Before I knew too much about it [being transgender], I kind of thought it [the negative message] was true. It used to make me question myself, and I always felt a lot of guilt, and I just felt like, "Why can't I just be normal?" Sometimes I had a lot of self-doubt. I thought, "Did something happen to me to make me like this" and "what if I'm really not what I think I am?" And it was just very scary thinking like that, because it just made me feel very insecure and lost. (Rood *et al.*, 2017, pp.9–10)

This quote illustrates the distrust of one's own feelings and thoughts and the alienation from the norm that are established by consistent incongruent and shaming mirroring.

Rochat (2009) says: "It is constitutive of the human psyche to have *others in mind*" (p.17). It should therefore not be unreasonable that when a person is figuring out their gender that how others see and interact with them should be important. In some clinical moments, it is useful to ask "What if you were on a desert island, how would you feel comfortable?" in order to remove the aspects of social pressure on the decision. In reality though, at some point when we leave our apartments, we are our genders with other people. Self-consciousness allows us to reflect on ourselves as well as think about how others see us, which functions as a reflective loop throughout our thoughts; ultimately, self-knowledge is a social process (Rochat, 2009). It is a social process since it always includes the fear of rejection by others.

Gender expression is a signal to others of who we see ourselves to be and a demand to be seen that way by others. We use our gender to attract potential partners. In the face of potential humiliation by others, one will feel paralyzed if shame has already taken root. How do we work to untangle shame's hold on the individual?

Amodeo and colleagues (2015) found higher rates of secure attachment in their non-clinical sample of Italian trans adults. Their study concluded that secure attachment enabled these folks to have a more positive trans identity, whereas the inverse was found in insecure attachment styles. The insecure group prioritized "passing" and thus experienced more shame (i.e. internalized transphobia). Therefore, the ability to incorporate transness as a positive identity trait as opposed to a liability will promote better emotional health.

How else do we overcome shame? We get angry. Anger is many times the antidote to the depressive, shameful position. Anger is a more adaptive reaction to transphobia since it may protect against internalizing it and bring an ability to recognize transphobia as wrong, as a societal ill not a personal one (Rood *et al.*, 2017). This relates to the social model of disability, where impairment is distinguished from the social oppression that creates disability, which will be explored in detail in Chapter 5.

This is simple to write but complicated to execute in session. Let's take for example a middle-aged adult who has asked her family to use different pronouns for her now. A person whose family dynamics and cultural background are that the children (even adult children) do not have the right to correct the parents or have their own feelings about a situation will obviously have a difficult time recognizing anger, articulating it in session and then being able to articulate it to the parents. In some cultures, or family systems, the individual does not have a right to her anger. Her internalized transphobia becomes compounded by superego edicts of silence.

It may be gentler clinically to start with compassion and empathy, for herself and her parents. The primary task of the therapist is not to diagnose but to be available as a good-enough mirror. To reflect: how hard it must be for her to hear her old name and pronoun, looking for how she does not feel recognized by her parents; how it must be hard for her parents to adjust (hard in the beginning, but if it has been years since asking for affirming pronouns, it is much harder not to see the parents as not making an effort). This must be done with substantial acknowledgment that it is inherently unfair to the trans person.

Another intervention to reduce shame was found in a 2009 study: certain gestures help to undo shame, such as gifts, nicknames, and clothing of the affirmed gender which mean a great deal to TGNC children (Koken, Bimbi & Parsons, 2009). These are simple direct expressions that loved ones can execute which can cut through shame.

Music therapist Julie Lipson has created group work with trans and genderqueer people which embodies positive mirroring and reducing shame (2017; in press). In her groups are directives like the syllable circle (borrowed from Theatre of the Oppressed) or frittata game, where one group member says a sound or a word which the next person must use but with a different intonation. It keeps going around the circle and gesture is included as well. Or there may be a sound–movement–phrase directive after a prompt. The prompts range from silly to more vulnerable ones, such as "how people react to my gender." The group mirrors back the reaction. Then the group is asked to embody "how I respond when others react to my gender." Since most participants have been bullied or criticized because of their voice and/or gendered gestures, this group is positively mirroring them and holding space for their embodiment. It also reduces censorship, since participants begin to have fun.

The differential clinical qualities between shame and stigma

Shame and stigma are similar in that they both can be categorized as small "t" traumas (minor adverse events that are not acute), and big "T" traumas (i.e. rape, plane crash, etc.), which could accumulate into having a clinical effect on the individual. We will address trauma more extensively in Chapter 6.

Shame is differentiated from stigma in specific ways. Shame comes from the personal, introjected, dyadic mirroring of distorted messages; stigma is part of society's oppression which can provoke shame. Stigma is happening outside the individual. Shame is also understood to activate a person's hypothalamic-pituitary-adrenocortical (HPA) axis which can increase the release of cortisol (stress hormone) into the bloodstream (Dickerson, Gruenewald & Kemeny, 2004). Dickerson and colleagues found that cortisol responses were highest in social-evaluative threat where the individual has the least control, which they termed exposed failure. They define social-evaluative threat as judgment from another or society of one's self-identity or self-esteem. It is commonly understood that activation of the HPA axis to acute and chronic stress exposes the individual to poorer health outcomes.

This concept of exposed failure threat is particularly applicable when looking at DuBois and colleagues' work (2017) with trans men during their transition. In DuBois' (2012a) cross-sectional Transition Experience Study, he interviewed and collected biomarkers of stress and health from 65 trans men who were using testosterone as part of their transition (DuBois, 2012a, 2012b). These measures included salivary measures of diurnal cortisol levels (i.e. a marker of stress activation in the HPA system) which were then examined in relation to stigma experience and minority stresses identified through the interviews (DuBois *et al.*, 2017). Stressors identified in the interviews included measures of what he has termed "transitioning-identity stress" (referring to stress experiences when different social circles come together who may not all know about one's transition or trans identity), stress associated with coming out, gender-specific public bathroom stress and stress due to being misgendered. He then evaluated these stressors in comparison to stress activation with general stress using Cohen's (1988) perceived stress scale. Much of this stress is connected to one's ability to pass as one's affirmed gender. They found that men experiencing transition-identity stress and gender-specific public bathroom stress had higher waking cortisol levels, which was interpreted as anticipatory stress related to stigma risk (e.g. being called a woman in the men's bathroom). However, due to the retention of the normal rhythm of diurnal cortisol and a steeper slope towards normalized bedtime levels, they interpreted this to indicate healthy, robust emotional responses to minority stressors and stigma (DuBois *et al.*, 2017). To me this means that most people may feel stressed about public bathrooms, but the ones who have figured out how to cope better will be mentally and physically healthier.

This difference between minority stress, stigma and shame directs how we work with shame and stigma in session. As the therapist, I should not challenge or deny a patient's experience of stigma. How do we tease out what is realistic fear and what is shame (when many times it is a mixture), for instance when a trans woman patient is not leaving the house? Even if she feels she is not passing, it does her a disservice to postpone her life until that point, particularly if she will not "pass" the way she wants to in the future. But to minimize or deny her experience of being stared at on the subway is to deny the existence of stigma. One can work with her on reducing her shame in order to hold herself more confidently if/when it happens, and to notice that not everyone is staring and to smile at those people. If she can keep the shame in check by not attaching to the negative perceptions she is reading in those stares, then she can move back to an emotional baseline after the initial spike when she notices the stares. The fear is real and sometimes interventions needed are not found in the therapist's office, but in a self-defense class. Shame makes the stigma stick. As therapists (and people) we cannot stop stigma from happening (that is the long-term project of social justice) but we can effect change in the depths of shame. "I can safely move about the city" is a nice thought, but unless you go out and do it and don't get harassed, you won't believe it. It is recognition by repetition. Overcoming shame is in some ways similar to trauma work. One must have corrective experiences to provide the self with new evidence that the positive message is true. She recognizes herself as a citizen with the right to feel free to be in the world, that she is exceptional but not abnormal. And normal is akin to average and nothing average was ever really that interesting.

CHAPTER 4

Gender, Terminable and Interminable

As Freud (1937) understood with psychoanalysis, we can say the same for understanding gender; it is a lengthy business. How long will it take? And do we ever finish our gender? Freud related that psychoanalysis is not a process we can speed up. Understanding gender will not be hurried either. It also appears to be a continuous construction. What form that construction materializes as is unique to the individual. We talk about transition as a discrete period of time. Yes, that may be so for certain interventions, but the full spectrum of one's gender and body and behavior continue to take shape over the lifespan. At every stage of human development, gender can come into consideration for everyone. Just as cisgender bodies continue to change with the effects of hormones or aging over the lifespan, so too do trans bodies. One's feelings about one's gender or gender expression can change over one's lifespan as well; many a cis man or cis woman I have worked with has had complicated feelings about their gender when trying to conceive a child, or when they do not feel their body is as able as it used to be, and what any of that says about their sense of their masculinity or femininity. The expression of our gender shifts as one's body is affected by menopause or the natural lowering of testosterone, as well as with the influence of aging, maturity and culture. There can be a misunderstanding by some medical professionals (and the general public) of trans communities that fluidity and change are equal to instability. We know in psychology that the ability to tolerate ambiguity is a hallmark of mental health; we should be applying this to gender as well.

Now, in this period at the beginning of the 21st century, when we have dislocated the assessment of gender from the blunt instruments of genitals and chromosomes, we should be careful not to recreate a binary system of objective measurement of gender by other means. This runs in contrast to the messaging many trans people have internalized: if I can't "pass, I shouldn't transition" (Rood *et al.*, 2017, p.13). Trans people are always balancing how they feel internally with what is read by others externally. This is a complicated equation, which I call the algorithm of gender.

Gender as algorithm

Gender is a multidimensional aspect of consciousness related to intrapsychic, interpersonal, interoceptive and exteroceptive experiences. My algorithm is the formulation of gender equilibrium. Through my clinical work, it appears to me that there is a gender sum the individual works towards through clothes (which are included in one's body-schema) comportment, private and public bodily interventions,[1] social role and sexual role. They could be categorized as falling under body and behavior, internal and external, intrapsychic and interpersonal, interoceptive and exteroceptive. The elements of the equation are malleable as long as the sum is achieved through the interplay between gender identity and expression. This is not to say that the sum may not change

---

1   See Langer (2014) for further discussion of the public and private aspects of gender-affirming medical interventions.

over a person's lifetime as well. The point of this algorithm is not prediction but to demonstrate the complicated and nuanced elements that make up one's gender, which also supports unlocking gender from a binary.

The formulation of the gender algorithm is an individualized tool that can be used clinically or by any individual. It is not meant as an instrument to determine *for* a trans person what their gender is by some other person, be it medical, mental health, parent, etc. There are 33 aspects of experience that each have their own degrees of masculinity, femininity or neutrality and their own level of importance to the individual. Some of these aspects are in or out of the individual's control or in some instances will or will not be affected by an intervention. Let's take hips, for instance: a trans masculine person may hope that testosterone will narrow his hips, which it does for some, but it may not happen for him or happen enough. At this point some other element, such as clothing, may ameliorate it or not. Eventually, one may need to work through mourning the body as an imperfect project (Langer, 2014).

These are the different elements of gender that I have worked with in clinical practice; not all with every patient but some combination.

- a=skin
- b=stomach—visual
- ç=stomach—hunger/ appetite
- c=body hair
- d=facial hair
- e=jawline
- ë=hairline/forehead
- é=ovaries
- f=uterus
- g=musculature
- h=voice
- i=penis
- í=testicles
- j=neck
- k=shoulders

- l=hands
- m=hips
- n=chest
- o=buttocks
- ö=clitoris
- ò=vagina
- p=emotional sensitivity or the feeling of feeling
- q=sex drive
- r=clothes

- s=jewelry
- t=sexual role
- u=personal social role
- v=professional social role
- w=family role
- x=accessories
- y=haircut
- ž=tattoos
- z=other internal viscera

Or it could be illustrated as the following diagram:

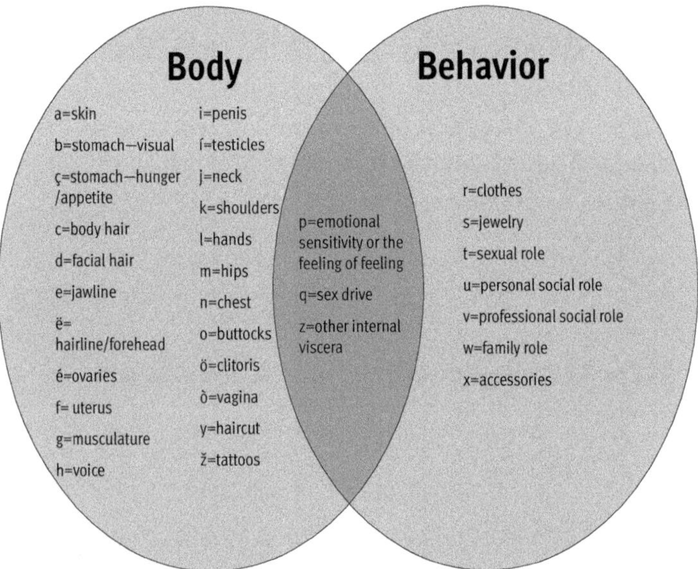

Figure 4.1 Gendered body and behavior elements

The overlapping area of the Venn diagram[2] captures the two areas which fall under both categories; it is both related to body and behavior. All of these elements have a place on a spectrum of masculinity or femininity. This ruler of femininity and masculinity has a center 0 where gender is neither feminine nor masculine, but gender neutral. This gender neutrality has two types of forms that can exist within it: one where feminine and masculine characteristics on either end of the spectrum create a highly signified combination of hyper-gendered elements and another where the elements of gender are all closer to the middle. Both of these may be called androgyny or genderqueer or gender non-binary, visibly queer or something else.

Obviously, many of these elements of gender are culturally specific, which is why this ruler is a subjective instrument to the individual. It is how the individual sees it—for instance, clothing as masculine or feminine—not the therapist or anyone else.

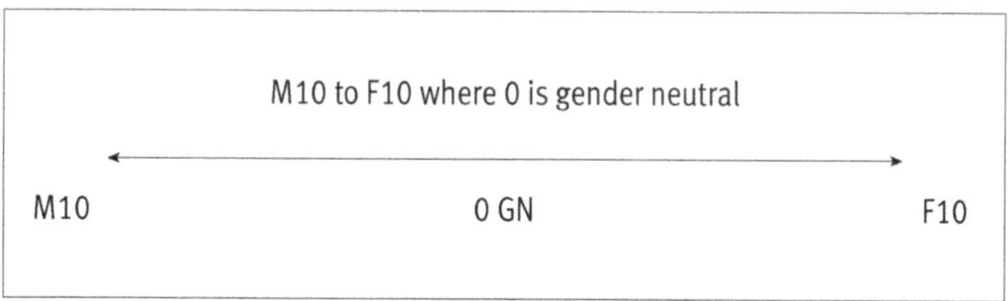

Figure 4.2 Extent of masculine, feminine and gender-neutral elements

---

2   This Venn diagram came about from my discussions with L. Zachary DuBois about my algorithm and his research into trans men's transition experiences. In his interviews with trans men, he developed a scale which divided gender experience into bodily and behavioral items, then asked trans men to indicate the level of importance and degrees of satisfaction with each characteristic (DuBois, 2012b). Independent of each other, we were beginning to formulate similar ideas. Together, we are now developing and validating an Embodiment of Gender Scale with fellow researcher Jae Puckett.

The second part of the variable is how important each of these aspects of gender is for any person ,which is represented as the coefficient: $M10^{10}$ =the most masculine and it is the most important.

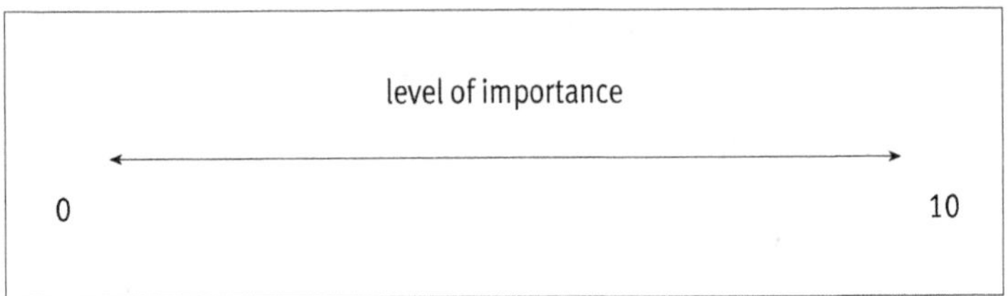

Figure 4.3 Level of importance of gendered element

For instance, genitals are important to almost every individual to varying degrees (not just transgender people, but trans people are demanded to explain their meaning to therapists and surgeons). Each variable of gender is represented by a letter, for instance, a (for skin) with a coefficient representing how masculine or feminine and an exponent (or power) for how important that element (the skin) is for the person. Therefore, if it is very important for a trans woman that her skin is very soft (more feminine); that variable would look like this: $F10a^{10}$.

The expression of gender would be represented as such: $F10a^{10} + F8b^{3} + F5c^{6}$ and so on, which equals the individual's gender identity. But gender is not that simple. These variables are not fixed, they interact with each other. So, a simple expression of addition is not sufficient. Certain variables take away or boost others depending on their location in proximity to each other. It may read more like this: $(F10a^{10}+F8b^{3}) + (F5c^{6}-M8d^{6}) +...=$ Gender Identity. If one's face has elements which are higher on the masculine scale than voice and haircut, a feminine voice and haircut may reduce the weight of those masculine features which then affects one's clothing and gestures, depending on where one wants to fall on the gender scale.

Every element of gender is a balanced alchemy towards individual gender balance. Not everyone needs the same level of masculinity or femininity. If one is working towards gender neutrality but has a strong masculine material body, then one may need more feminine clothing, mannerisms and voice to bring the needle to the middle. One patient of mine who was assigned female at birth was jealous of their partner who was assigned male at birth because it seemed easier for the partner to be read as genderqueer since, with a male body, simply (or not so simply) putting on a dress makes one recognized as gender transgressive.

Adam from *Trans Voices* captures this process for a trans man:

> It is easier to compensate for an absence but harder to suppress a presence. Every trans man does a spot of body mapping. I hated having breasts. They didn't fit with my sense of self. I viewed them as an unnecessary growth, and longed to return to the days of pre-puberty when I was flat-chested. Therefore, it was not a hard decision to have the lumps of fat removed. What was more difficult though was deciding whether I should take testosterone. I questioned if putting this chemical into my body was necessary for me to transition but knew there was no other means if I wanted to make my body look as masculine as possible. (Henry, 2017, p.102)

From his words, we can extrapolate that he already had the interoceptive feeling of a flat chest, but that other gendered elements were more elusive in deciding about testosterone.

This phenomenon can happen even when it is only gender-affirming clothing: "Then, when I throw off all that is the man and put on the woman externally, I can almost physically feel how the false, the violence, leaves me and disappears like a fog" (Hirschfeld, 1919/1991, p.214). The lifting of the fog is no less relevant today than it was almost 100 years ago in Germany when Magnus Hirschfeld described his patients. The relief of the fog leaving is the sensation of the reduction of free energy. The power of embodying one's experienced gender in affirming ways endorses how foundational gender is as a homeostatic emotion.

Let us use the analogy of temperature as a stand-in for gender when thinking about homeostatic emotion. With each thermal sensation (interoception) a homeostatic emotion (which can be pleasant or not) is provoked, which then initiates a regulatory motivation. For temperature, there are thermoregulatory automatic mechanisms internally (I begin to sweat) or externally (I take my sweater off), all directed towards energy efficiency. What is even more critical is that the feeling and motivation is context dependent (Strigo & Craig, 2016). This is exactly what is happening for gender. With each gendered sensation, a homeostatic emotion (gender dysphoria or congruence) is provoked, which initiates a regulatory motivation, such as more feminine clothing or binding or hormone treatment. DuBois and colleagues (2016) found that depression and anxiety were associated with lower levels of satisfaction with the aspects of the body and behavior which they rated as important. This points to emotional dysregulation in the gender system.

Next, let's address the importance of social context. For temperature, if you are giving a presentation, you know you will be nervous and thus sweatier, so you will generally wear your lightest suit. Or someone may need a more feminine outfit with breast enhancement when she is visiting her family in order to feel more embodied as a woman in the face of their struggle to see her authentic self. Within her own body and shape, in her own interoceptive sensations, her sense of her femininity feels more congruent within that hostile context that is not as reflective of her. Gendered choices are an embodied process, a type of allostasis (learning what works to feel equilibrium), that does not happen in a vacuum.

A non-binary patient of mine described their experience of finding gender alignment as analogous to upgrading your musical instrument. When you play with a cheaper, less well-made musical instrument, you learn how to compensate for its glitches to get the proper sound. Then when you advance enough and buy a better instrument, it is so much easier to sound good. I would add to this analogy that for some people it is upgrading their instrument, whereas for others it is switching instruments. Imagine you have been playing the oboe for many years but can never quite get your playing to a fluid place. You have to think about every note you play and can never lose yourself in the music. Then you are given a saxophone and you can play it almost instinctually. It is not a forced process of playing. This is what it feels like when one is living in one's affirmed gender.

The feat of taking action on even one of these elements can give a person more of a sense of ownership over their body and self. I have had multiple patients talk about how the act of getting a tattoo (even if it wasn't particularly gendered) enhanced their ability to feel connected to their bodies in a positive way. Tattoos are also a (mostly) permanent means to alter one's body in a creative and productive way. This can help one to overcome the stigma connected to altering one's body, and to feel that one has the right to change one's body. It increases body ownership.

The algorithm is a useful model—particularly for gender-queer, agender, non-binary and androgynous identities and presentations—instead of thinking about gender as a wholesale endeavor. This also comes out of practicing in the U.S.A. where each gendered intervention had been completely self-financed up until recently (in some states insurance now covers trans healthcare), unlike in some other countries where once you are diagnosed with gender dysphoria there is a clear path that subsidizes all options related to medical transition. The financial burden of transition used to force people to have to choose between necessary interventions, thus developing a hierarchy of needs. If someone was sure about top surgery, he may have actually chosen to start testosterone, since it was more affordable and accessible while he saved up for surgery. It will be important to retain the individuality of interventions as we increase access to them.

Gender relativity

The size-contrast illusion is a perceptual trick called the "Titchener circles" (or "Ebbinghaus") illusion (Aglioti, DeSouza & Goodale, 1995). Both the inner circles are actually the same size, but the size of the other circles in relation to them changes your visual perception of them (interestingly, it does not change your tactile perception of them since if you reach for them, your fingers separate to the accurate size).

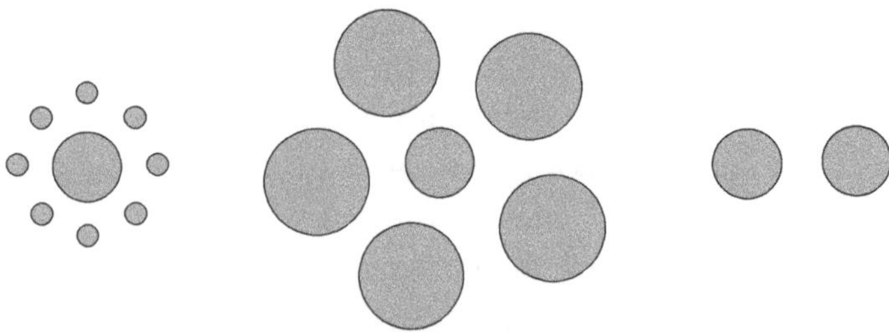

Figure 4.4 Titchener circles

The juxtaposition of these circles illustrates how the relationship of objects to each other changes our perception of them. It is a simplistic illustration of how the elements of gender are perceived and understood by others in how they relate to each other. If a trans man's shoulders, back and chest are more muscular (masculine), then his more neutral voice gets read as male. Certainly, some of these elements on their own are weighted more masculine or feminine. A small amount of facial hair goes a long way towards masculinity, or breast development towards femininity.

The relativity of gender components is processed intrapsychically and is subject to interpersonal dynamics. Just as Einstein (1961) taught us that perceptions of space and time are relative to the perceiver's velocity, so too are gendered elements perceived differently depending on the observer's orientation towards gender. Trans people know that others are calculating their characteristics. Clerks in stores make a gendered judgment call when they look, listen (add it up) and then say "sir" or "ma'am." It means something to be recognized in the world. It is unfair and unrealistic for clinicians to say to trans people that they should not be worried about what other people think. We all are concerned about how others perceive us. No one likes to be misgendered; it is just that trans people have to contend with it on a more persistent basis.

If we think of the formula to include other's perceptions, it can either divide or multiply one's recognition. Other people's recognition of one's gender expression as one's gender identity could be called the Intensity of the Relational Field. One's gendered elements can be divided (by a negative reaction) or multiplied by how intense and accurate other's perceptions are.

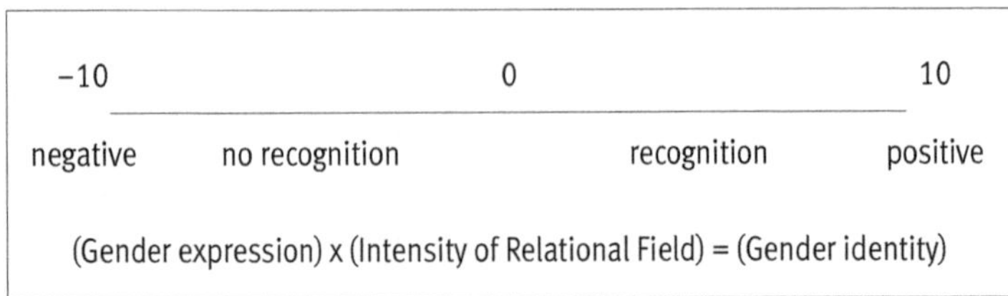

Figure 4.5 Intensity of the Relational Field

For instance, some patients have reported to me that when they return to their hometown in a more conservative area of the country than New York City, they are not misgendered there. Their gender expression in New York is seen as androgynous (since more variety of gender expression is recognized) whereas in Oklahoma their expression of gender falls firmly into the binary. If a person is wearing a dress, then it is certainly a woman, no matter how tall she is, but in San Francisco others may not make that assumption.

The algorithm and gender's relativity are illustrated by the classic Overlay Study by Kessler and McKenna (1978). They showed participants in the study overlays of a person in various levels of dress and undress with multiple attributes of masculinity and femininity. They had 96 different combinations. One example from it is when you show people a picture of a masculine naked body without a penis (think the sculpture David without the genitals), it is identified as a man. Then if you show a picture of a feminine naked body (think Venus De Milo with arms) with a penis, it is also identified as a man. The breasts and long hair do not outweigh the penis. They concluded that the world's perceptions are weighted towards the masculine; they thought this explained why it is easier for trans men to "pass" than trans women.

Post-interventions

What I have described so far is the process prior to (the figuring it out) and during transition (some decisions have been made). Next let us turn to the unexpected shifts which may occur for some people once interventions have been accomplished. In my clinical experience, I have witnessed how certain elements which felt fixed for the individual shifted once other elements were reaching the masculinity or femininity quotient. The other use of this algorithm, which is what initially sparked the idea for me, was hearing how people's experience of their gender adjusted after a medical intervention which began to change their body. The shift in their body as more affirming of their gender identity sometimes shifted other gendered behavior or preference, consciously and unconsciously. For example, one patient felt less constricted in his mannerisms (that were read as feminine) after his voice deepened enough. He had felt that changing his gestures to stereotypical masculine norms felt congruent for him prior to testosterone. It surprised him that he felt comfortable with some manner of femininity, now that his voice had a higher degree of masculinity. Or the trans woman who felt she did not need to wear as feminine clothing since her body began to shift into a more feminine frame from hormone treatment. Or the trans woman who after facial feminization surgery felt like she wanted to wear fewer dresses since her gender was more recognizable on her face, whereas before she needed to wear very feminine clothing in order to feel comfortable in herself and to be read correctly. The formulation of their gender was more complex and nuanced than just stereotypically male or female. Or, for instance, a patient who, once his physical traits were reaching the level of masculinity he wanted, felt safe to explore what he felt were feminine positions/ behavior with sexual partners. Erica Rand pointedly illustrates the inter-relational nature of gender in her piece about hips:

> When it comes to hips, all of the following can matter: the right belt, the right hormones (endogenous, exogenous); stomach, shoulders, thighs, and butt; muscle, food, training; the uniform, the outfit; spandex, padding; disposable income for all of the above; ideas about essence, affinity, and culture working their way separately or together. (Rand, 2014, p.99)

This list should also include race, ethnicity and culture, since what is deemed attractive or acceptable is influenced by these forces.

One patient was surprised at how his motivation to train at the gym had gone down after phalloplasty. He had always been dedicated to working out so it surprised him that returning to the gym post-surgery, while still enjoyable, did not have the same urgency. In talking it through, he understood this shift as previously needing to feel as strong as possible prior to surgery to feel a certain level of masculinity, but now that his body reflects his masculinity more fully, he does not need the workout to express it for him.

Another example is how behavior is understood based on how someone's gender is read. One patient of mine was a salesperson prior to transition (he was perceived as a "butch lesbian"). He was a top seller—part of his success he attributed to the fact that men were not threatened by him as a lesbian and women felt comfortable talking with another woman. Then he began hormone treatment and quickly was being read as male. His sales behavior did not change but his successful sales plummeted. His same behavior was somehow off-putting to men and women when enacted by a male-appearing body. It ended his career in sales. He did not want to change his demeanor, so he had to adjust his expectations of how he would be perceived by others.

Algorithm in action

The following excerpt from a patient's email to me captures the struggle to parse out what one is actually feeling (or giving into social messages) and how that fits into one's social encounters. They were communicating this through email since they were having difficulty verbally articulating these thoughts about gender in person and kept feeling an urgency to talk about more immediate concerns (like job and relationship issues) with me. The email served to kick-start a more in-depth exploration of gender within session.

This passage illustrates how being and knowing one's gender do not exist in a void. They are related to one's psychic health, personality traits, relationships with others, and how one is trying to change in therapy. We do not work on anything in isolation in psychotherapy. The whole person is there with all their difficulties and history and strengths and nuances. This patient is a 30-year-old, white, non-binary-identified trans person, who uses the pronoun they, and who initially sought treatment for mood/affect difficulties. They are very bright and have been working recently on whether they need masculinizing interventions to feel comfortable in their body. We have been working together for three years, twice a week. We worked through the various themes in the email in subsequent sessions and when I showed them this chapter.

The email captures the patient's struggle to know what is going to be right for them. It also illustrates how various gender elements intersect with non-gender struggles and how a person sorts through them.[3]

---

3   I have not edited this email in order to retain its integrity so there may be grammatical mistakes as it is a stream of consciousness.

I have this thing about flatness… I've been concerned about at least since puberty-ish. It is one of the things that makes it difficult to know what I want because flatness based desires and gender based desires are easily conflated. When I was in high school I had a strong desire to be flat chested and was generally attracted to boyish women… I just thought it looked better on women. I used to put my elbows in my waist and lay my arms down at my hip bones and if any skin touched my arm in between I thought I was too fat (which was almost the whole time). I actually did that again recently to see that I had gained weight. Even with scratching and picking (not gendered) particularly in the day time which I'm picking up again, I feel compelled by the desire to be smooth. I'm okay with flat moles and freckles but I feel really awkward about raised moles (also not gendered) on myself and other people.

So when I want top surgery, do i want it because I don't want breasts or because I want to be flat? When I want to take T, do I want to because it will help me take a more masculine form or because it will fill out my waist and de-curve my thighs?

Sometimes I'm really afraid of looking male. I don't know if that's because I'm not male or because I'm afraid of having things I want.

Sometimes I feel really happy when I look like a man. I don't know if it is any different from when I feel happy for pulling off a woman look—pride at my ability to pass… stealth-ness. Of course when I think I look like a man I don't actually. I know cuz other people tell me. When I look in the mirror I see something other people don't see. Something I don't see when I look at a picture. I don't want to look like a woman dressed in men's clothing I want to look like a man.

Sometimes I think if my body were more androgynous then i could make it look more like a man and make it look like a passable woman too. I don't know how to do that though. I don't think there's anything that gives me enough control for that to actually happen.

Sometimes I don't care how I look as long as I don't look like a male/female mashup (this is gross language).[4] If i can look like a proper woman then that's fine and I do now as long as I can learn how to dress myself again. When I put my hair up in a pony tail and my bangs are down I think I look like a very nice girl.

When I'm at home by myself, I think my body is fine. I think I am tall and thin for a botticelli. I think I am elegant in my own way. I think I know how to command attention. I don't like wearing underwear of any kind. I only wear enough clothing for physical comfort. I don't like wearing scanty feminine things though because I feel big and clunky in them. That's a regular woman feel. But I don't need flatness when I'm naked at home by my self, only when others look at me or I put clothes on.

I haven't been wearing the packer because in the underwear I got for it, it tilts forward and its not against my body really at all and then i feel embarrassed. But when I'm at home [my partner] is usually at home and it is easy to feel embarrassed when I don't know how they feel about it but they seemed to think it was weird.

When I'm around other humans, if I'm not wearing anything on my chest under my shirt I feel very exposed. If I'm in public but with friends I prefer to go that way. I like to bind but I can't get flat so I'm losing my interest in it.

When I think about wearing a dress after top surgery or breast reduction, i think it will look weird either way. I think

---

4   The patient and I talked specifically about how this reflects the conflict between conscious, intellectual understanding of the transphobic nature of this comment and the guttural, emotional and shame-based attachment to this line of thinking when one is really struggling to understand oneself.

I'm in reasonable proportion now. I have no desire to wear dresses now.

But all of these things are in direct conflict with one another. I can't imagine any version of myself that would allow of those feelings to be satisfied. I can't think of a #BodyGoal. So how on earth could I decide on doing anything to alter my body? I do not think I could handle acne and balding. It would be worth it if it would resolve body anxiety but how can i know that?

The only thing I know I want is a dick. And I think clit growth would be sufficient *if* it even happened on T which there is no guarantee. Right now I feel like I want top surgery and I want to be on T but I have this feeling like maybe I'm being really essentialist like everything needs to happen at once or I'll feel even worse if I'm (i know this is wrong but this is really inside me somewhere) part-male and part-female. (Personal communication, 8/4/2017)

The first paragraph addresses the patient's struggle with compulsive self-harm behaviors and how they make meaning of it and cope with it. Then it shifts to trying to find the reasons why they want masculinizing interventions. But why is one reason more legitimate than another? This inevitably arises in most people's exploration of gender; is what I need or want legitimate enough to go through with this intervention?

They continue to explore the conundrum of being non-binary and finding some satisfaction in presenting well as masculine and/or feminine and searching within the self as to where they felt most authentic in those gendered embodiments. For the patient, presenting well meant looking good/attractive—to self and others. Then they were particularly working through the shame attached to being a "mashup," and knowing "mashup" is internalized transphobia but still having difficulty not being influenced by it. Additionally, all of the work around gender for this patient is hamstrung by the patient's belief that they do not deserve to be happy (which is an improvement from not believing they had a right to live).

The email ends on one of a few comments directly expressing the patient's shame and illustrates how the patient is aware of it but still has a hard time not believing it. It also captures how the various gendered elements are interrelated to each other and do not really function in isolation. The struggle to understand what is a gendered feeling and what are other personal issues (like allowing oneself to be happy) are also so clearly delineated here. When we reflected on it further, after they read this chapter, they said I should highlight more the differences between societal perceptions and internalized feelings about women's bodies which are so pervasive and distinguish those from personal gendered feelings. The impact of being socialized as a girl in a society that promotes body shame in women is an extraction that takes some herculean effort. The dissection of internalized misogyny, transphobia, body shame and then one's actual gendered feelings takes time and patience to examine and excise each of these layers and how they interrelate with each other. In therapy, we are never working on one thing at a time; humans are not that neatly divided up. It is also technically and practically difficult to distinguish shame from repulsion. Shame of what I want versus repulsion of what I do not want. These can sensationally feel similar. I think this patient's words illustrate this conflict well.

Since this patient is a very thoughtful and academic person, they can easily understand and argue many perspectives, which can cloud what they can viscerally know from their own perception of their body and feelings. They explained how they need to come up with their own gender, which would not be a gender that is male or female or a gender that is in relation to the binary.

Another aspect I want to highlight is the patient's certainty about having a penis. This interoceptive signal was the strongest, whereas the other bodily aspects were harder for the patient to read. In keeping with the research on interoceptive training discussed in the beginning of this book, in order to hear subtler signals, one should start with the more obvious ones. Weeks before this email, after the patient had verbalized multiple times that they were only sure about needing a penis, I suggested the patient buy a packer. Why should they wait to reduce the free energy related to that gendered aspect? Why not access a packer, even if one is not being read as male? In the email, the packer is not working completely but they still feel sure about that element. There is also the embarrassment the patient feels if the packer could be noticed by others that needs to be worked through. In the current standards of care for bottom surgery, this patient would not be able to access phalloplasty (since they had not been on testosterone or lived as a man for a year) but they can still access the compromise accommodation.

In my clinical practice, most people do not begin their exploration of gender as deciding between male or female (man or woman). The process begins with a feeling about certain behaviors or gender expressions, such as clothes or hair; or a feeling about a certain body part. There is the difficulty of how to read one's own signals. It may not be until they know that there is such a thing called transgender that their feelings will start to make sense. It is analogous to the sine-wave speech listening task. Sine-wave speech is a stripped-down version of a sentence, leaving only a rough outline of the sentence.[5] There are two sound samples:

---

5   Go to www.lifesci.sussex.ac.uk/home/Chris_Darwin/SWS to hear the examples.

one that is distorted and one that has the clearly spoken sentence. The trick is then to listen to the first distorted one again. Once one has a prediction of what is being said, the clear sentence can be "heard" in the first sound sample. This phenomenon is what it feels like for a trans person when they begin to think that maybe these sensations they are feeling may be articulated as transness. Their internal feelings start to make sense; they can "hear" the message now, even if it is still a bit garbled. Then post-intervention one's body has the clarity of the second sound sample: the distortion is gone.

The language of how to identify comes much later in the process, which is why the burden on trans and gender diverse patients to have a particular identity prior to a medical intervention is plainly wrong and clinically unsound. It is unsound, because, for example, many people cannot know fully how they feel about masculinization/ feminization until they actually experience their body with exogenous hormones. A patient may know they want a lower voice and more body hair but are unsure if they identify as a trans man; it is not until their body becomes more masculine that they can really feel and understand their identity better. Identity follows the understanding and execution of the above gendered facets. Illustrative of this are the identity breakdowns identified in the 65 interviews with trans men in DuBois' (2012a) Trans Experience Study (image below used with permission from the author). These suggest that when you allow people to answer how they want and do not provide exact boxes, the spectrum of identities can more easily be revealed. The variety of identities and variation of people's need for and experience of gendered interventions highlight what the algorithm proves: gender is discrete and idiosyncratic.

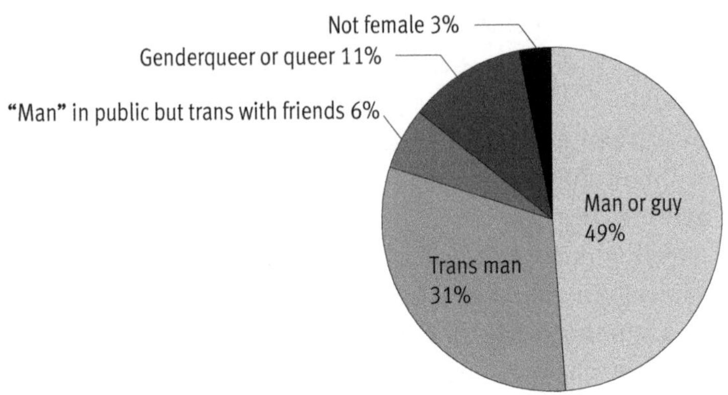

Figure 4.6 Variety of gender identities
(*Image used with permission of the author L. Zachary DuBois. This breakdown demonstrates the variety within the identity of trans men.*)

In my sessions, we are delicately handling each of these gender elements. We question and re-question our assumptions and perceptions. Then the patient needs to take action between sessions, searching and researching, experimenting with each element's varying powers and the combinations between them. It is an alchemy. The right gender formula is about creativity, transformation and balance.

The initial application of the algorithm was to demonstrate to my patients (and other clinicians) that gender is not a wholesale endeavor. We may or may not want to adjust aspects of our body and behavior to only one side of the gender spectrum. Equilibrium and comfort are more about the combination that create the sum of our gender.

Many times, patients need help understanding that they do not need to identify any particular way in order for us to explore aspects of their body they may need to change. Regardless of how a trans trajectory is laid out in the Standards of Care (SOC7) or other literature, this is usually not very useful in the consulting room

(WPATH, 2011). The therapist is wise to have no attachment to what aspects of gender go with each other; they will always be surprised.

Rachlin's (2018) clinical experience reinforces this point. Some of her patients require medical interventions (surgery or hormones) to affirm their experienced gender but they do not need or want to socially transition. One patient was assigned male at birth and was still living as male into middle age. He was married to a woman, with children and was a community leader, all of which he felt certain he would have lost if he socially transitioned. He chose not to socially transition but his need for gender affirming medical intervention was still important to his survival. Another of her patients was assigned female at birth and lived as a butch woman. She knew she needed top surgery but had no interest in living as a man. These patients deserve support in acquiring these interventions regardless of identity.

Transition, terminable and interminable

The semantic title of transition is too broad and heavily laden with meaning and it may not apply to every trans person. It also implies a discrete period of time, which may not be accurate to most people's experience. Identity is constantly in transition, being renegotiated depending on our social circumstances (Rochat, 2009). Rochat also believes that everyone's identity is actually in the transitional moments between self-concepts. If we look through an Eriksonian lens, so that at each developmental stage we decide what kind of person we will be, those who are flexible fare better. The decisions and definitions concerning transition interventions can only be made by the subjects experiencing the sensations of gender and how much they matter to them in the context in which they are living in the present moment. The algorithm does not rely on identity, which hopefully will work towards the algorithm enduring through the rapidly and creatively changing ways people identify. This formulation places the power of gender back into feeling and thus relieving the pressure of semantic articulation. There is never going to be a "gold standard of prediction" to determine who "should or should not" transition, because the very premise that an outside observer can decide what someone else's gender is is fundamentally flawed. It also comes from a stance that the feelings of being transgender are an illness and thus need to be diagnosed by a mental or physical health professional.

Through my clinical work, using this algorithm (with the patient, or just keeping it in mind myself as a clinical stance), has worked as a route into gender exploration without knowing the end point. We all need to be patient with our own process. As Thomas Page McBee (2014) says in his memoir, "I could only be my own man; I didn't have a choice" (p.163). The definition of what man meant was unique to him.

Decision making—conscious and unconscious

Paradoxically, through all this conscious negotiating of gender; there is the important element of unconscious decision making. According to Unconscious Thought Theory (UTT), we make complex decisions more accurately through unconscious processing because the unconscious does not have the same limit of capacity as conscious thought (Dijksterhuis *et al.*, 2006). Dijksterhuis and collegues say that a larger amount of information can be integrated unconsciously than consciously. They termed it the "deliberation-without-attention" hypothesis.

One of their experiments was comparing decision making in shopping at Ikea (complex) or Bijenkorf (simple-Macy's type store). Conscious thinkers were more satisfied with their purchases from Bijenkorf, whereas unconscious thinkers were more satisfied with their Ikea ones (it could also have been that not deliberating gets one out of Ikea faster, which is always more satisfying).[6] In a simplistic way, this is in some way the "sleep on it method" as we process learning and information during rapid eye movement (REM) sleep, which is also to say, trust your gut. It has been my experience with some patients that we will consciously and rationally be working over whether or not to take action on a gendered intervention until that one day when they walk in and say, "Yes, I'm doing it." And when I ask what clinched it for them, they reply, "I just *know* it *feels right now*."

It can be excruciating to feel like you do not know your gender or even more unbearable to know it and be delayed in taking action. My theory of gender as a foundational aspect of consciousness and this algorithm make clear how the level of complexity down to the atomic level and the individuality of the multiple combinations of these elements makes gender anything but binary or static.

When we think about how we feel these various aspects of our bodies, it is interesting to ponder what the representation of our body is on the surface in the brain. The more sensitive (a high concentration of neurons) an area is, the more it is represented in the brain. Is this representation different for transgender people? Wilder Penfield, the pioneering neurosurgeon from the beginning of the last century, discovered what is called the sensory

---

6   Not everyone agrees on the validity of UTT; see—Chrabaszcs & Doughtery (2012).

homunculus, which is the sensory map of the cortical surface of the brain. An illustration of it looks like a little man whose different areas of the body are drawn in proportion to their sensory importance (i.e. the lips and hands are very large compared to the rest of the body) (Ramachandran & Blakeslee, 1998). Interestingly, the genitals are not particularly represented larger than actual size. This is possibly another reinforcement of how genitals are usually not the most important aspect of someone's transition. Penfield opened up the skull to discover this map; these days we can use magnetoencephalography (MEG). In two hours, you can have a map of your body. Does the level of importance of each of these elements map to our cortical surface? Are certain body parts important to us because we feel them more? We do not know, yet.

Courage

Courage is ontological; we cannot exist without it (Tillich, 1952). Trans people are ontologically compelled to confront their gender—like McBee says, "I didn't have a choice" (2014, p.163). Rollo May (1975) instructs us that one becomes fully human by the choices one makes and the commitment to act on those choices; this is unlike other beings in nature who act on impulse or instinct. An acorn just becomes an oak tree, no courage is needed (May, 1975). Transition is not a passive activity; it takes action and more action. It does not just transform bodily characteristics but demands one to ask for what one needs from others, to stand up for oneself, to enact and embody self-worth.

Creativity is fundamentally about discovering new forms (May, 1975). May goes on to say that this *"bringing something new into being"* defines it as art (p.39, italics in original). Trans people are the true artists of their beings. The creative endeavor is constantly a dialectical process between the self and others; it is never totally within the self. The decisions people make about their gender expression follow the same rules. As I have shown, there is much internal, subjective understanding that needs to be accomplished to know one's gender, but then that gender must be lived in the world. How one executes one's gender is in consideration of that world.

"To see myself, I have to trust my gaze." My patient (who also sent the email) said this to me when we were embarking on exploring their gender. It beautifully encapsulates how knowing one's gender is not just about seeing, but about believing oneself. The patient is also saying succinctly that the introjected gaze of the other, the incongruently mirrored gaze of the primary others, will need to be let go. The internalized voice which contributed to the false self development will need to fall away for the true self to be seen.

A different patient and I were discussing the exceptional position trans people are in—they have the opportunity to experience the world in ways others cannot. He went on to say how trans people have a different relationship to the truth than cis people. They must listen to their own intuition without any visible or social reinforcement. There is a development in the ability to trust oneself over others and to question assumptions. One must develop one's own philosophy of knowledge. This is the creative leap towards acceptance that leads to decision.

CHAPTER 5

Accommodating for Bodies

What can disabilities studies teach us about how to understand trans experience? How do we have sex with a body that does not function or look or reach in the way we need it to? How can we position our bodies when parts are in the way or missing? What is the psychotherapist's role in exploring these aspects of the body and the psychological barriers? Is a trans body disabled when it comes to sex? What should we do when it is physically impossible to have sex in an ego-syntonic way? My attempt here is to illustrate the overlap between trans and disability particularly in the sphere of sex and sexuality through interdisciplinary lenses.

Both these communities[1] are haunted by the concept of normalcy. "The norm" was not in the consciousness of English until 1840–1860. It was preceded by the notion of "the ideal" (Davis, 2013), namely that the gods were the ideal: "in a culture with an ideal form of the body, all members of the population are below the ideal" (Davis, 2013, p.2) and then average is allowed to be flawed. This is to say that prior to a norm being imposed, if only the gods are ideal it lets the rest of us off the hook. But now we have what Davis would call the "tyranny of the norm"

---

1   I acknowledge that this is a false division, as there are many people who are trans and have a disability. My discussing it as two discrete categories is illustrative and not meant to erase anyone's experience.

(Davis, 2013, p.3). Transness, and particularly visible transness, applies pressure to this sensibility of normality with the size and shape of trans bodies, just as people with disabilities are scrutinized concerning their bodies.

Eugenics

To place this in a historical context, we need to look back to eugenics and its effect on culture. The aim of eugenics was statistically norming and non-norming the population and then using that to eliminate the outliers, perfecting the body (Davis, 2013). It was a drive to improve the genetics of human kind which was ultimately discredited through its association with Nazism. Still, this was a time in history that has had far-reaching effects on how we think about nonconforming bodies. Even after that, there has been forced sterilization of disabled people and trans people. For example, in some countries (such as France, Italy, Turkey) you are required to have sterilization surgery to change your gender on national documents (Pyne, 2017; World Health Organization, 2014).

The intolerance of visible transness within and outside of the trans community is part of the eugenics legacy. There will never be equality for trans people if the visibility of trans existence remains an insult to society. This can be seen in trans-health on a variety of levels. For instance, in a presentation at the Trans Studies Conference in 2016, Chris Straayer gave an example concerning trans surgeries and depth of the neo-vagina. He discussed trans women who are asking surgeons for a particular depth of their vaginas and are being told that they do not need that kind of depth since the amount of depth needed for penile pleasure is around six to seven inches. The "norm" as stated by the surgeon was without regard for the individuals' subjectivity. There was no acknowledgment by some physicians that a woman may privilege her pleasure over that of her male partners, or that her partners may be women, or a myriad of other reasons she may desire varying depth in her vagina.

The medical model of disability is the same model used for transness: there is an illness that needs to be cured. The social model of disability, initiated by Michael Oliver, seeks to challenge ableism by defining the limitations experienced by disabled people as originating from the barriers set in motion by oppressive systems, and suggesting that if these social problems were addressed there would be less discrimination in access and accommodations. Therefore, there is a distinction between impairment and disability, between illness and disability. Oliver (2009) theorized impairment as the "lacking part or all of a limb or having a defective limb, organism or mechanism of the body" (p.22). Disability, on the other hand, is "the disadvantage or restriction of activity caused by a contemporary social organization which takes no or little account of people who have physical (and/or cognitive/developmental/ mental) impairments and thus excludes them from the mainstream of society" (UPIAS and the Disability Alliance, 1976, p.14). Lack of access also serves to render disabled people invisible since if you cannot physically arrive at a location, you are not seen. Shakespeare (1992) succinctly sums up the difference as between (impaired) bodies and (disabling) societal conditions.

Oliver began his thinking about disability after a spinal cord injury in adulthood. He felt and was told that he was unemployable. What interests me about this is how his experience overlaps with that of trans people. Your body is out of the norm, but the disability comes from the social structure built around those bodies. The differently embodied trans person contends with the disabling societal stigma and loss of access to spaces and resources, but for some people, their body is also experienced as impaired.

This is particularly relevant to sex, but also in relation to public accommodations.

Tremain (2006) argues that in contesting the model of disability, even through the social model, one is still upholding that structure. She says that impairment has been a part of disability throughout history. Tremain feels that to talk about impairment/disability serves only to uphold the oppressive system (one example being disability benefits from the government). She rallies for a shift from an "I am" position to an "I want" position. This is a positive, active stance which is certainly helpful in psychotherapy.

The theory that may capture this constellation of experience is the "composite model of disability" conceptualized by Baril (2015, p.60), which takes into account both of these theories of Oliver and Tremain. His model addresses the idea that even if all oppressive systems and barriers are removed (no disability), there needs to be acknowledgment that some personal suffering might still exist (some impairment). Baril solidly places trans communities and persons with disabilities on a similar plane. No amount of social justice will remove all suffering for many trans people; unlike LBG communities, there is some inherent suffering internally for some trans people. This is similar to (but of course not the same) as someone with cerebral palsy who has pain when they walk (Baril, 2015). Even if you build accessible buildings, this person will still have some degree of suffering, just like if a workplace ungenders the bathrooms, it does not end the suffering of some trans folks confronted with incongruent genitalia at every visit to the bathroom.

This is also similar to the concept of Scott's (1988) so-called collective affinity, this theory being that the identities given to a group are used by society to oppress them. Ultimately it is that the "problem is the way normalcy is constructed" (Davis, 2013, p.1). Disability and trans share histories of medicalization and institutionalization, but despite gender dysphoria being a medical psychiatric diagnosis, it is excluded from the American with Disabilities Act (Spade, 2003), insurance company carve-outs (Bauer *et al.*, 2009) and sick-leave policies (Shelley, 2008). These policies have tangible impacts on the lives of trans people. Cis men who are missing a penis or have a micropenis can receive prosthetics as medical supplies because they are considered disabled, whereas trans men who need these same prosthetics do not. Under these policies, these identical prosthetics when needed by trans men are now considered sex toys and are not covered by insurance. Prosthetics or tool-use are an essential component of humanity and work as a bridge between the body and environment (Clark, 1999; De Preester & Tsakiris, 2009; Heidegger, 1927). This is lost on insurance companies and is a major therapeutic obstacle. If we look at men with Disorders of Sex Development (DSD), we know that having a micropenis has a negative effect on sexual self-confidence (Bouvattier *et al.*, 2006). This had been a justification for surgery on men with DSD as infants; that being a man requires a penis which can penetrate a vagina—if not, the child was "made female" (Wilkerson, 2012).

Trans people are also denied aid because of the myth/prejudice that trans people's impairment is their own fault. If a vaginoplasty has multiple complications, these women hear, "Well, you decided to have the surgery." Or the experience of a trans man who after top surgery is angry because he has lost a nipple, but is told he should just be happy his chest is flat. This is similar to someone with mobility issues being told they should just be happy that there is a space for their wheelchair in the back of the theater, even though they may not be able to see very well from there.

Possibly the only alternative to phalloplasty available today is penis transplant, but this surgery is not offered to trans men. Jeffrey Kahn, a bioethicist at Johns Hopkins contemplated penis transplants for trans men in a *New York Times* article:

> Once this becomes public and there's some sense that this is successful and a good therapy, there will be all sorts of questions about whether you will do it for gender reassignment, what do you say to the donor? A 23-year-old wounded in the line of duty has a very different sound than somebody who is seeking gender reassignment. (Quoted in Grady, 2015)

What is that different sound? He is implying something which he feels is so obvious that he does not have to name it. Is it that a man who has lost his penis only in war is worthy of donation? Or is it likely he is saying that trans men are not really "men," so how could he possibly imagine asking someone to donate a penis to a "woman"? He fails to understand that the importance of having a penis to a male identity is the same for cis men as it is for some trans men. Both men are impaired; the trans man is actually more disabled because he does not have access to the same accommodations as the cis man.

The experience of prosthetics can be a point of comradery between amputees and trans people. As Murray (2004) points out:

> Fitting a dead thing to your live body is and always will be an imperfect process. The most critical thing is establishing a good fit. Unfortunately, your body will change over time, so a good fit today may not feel as good tomorrow, then it will feel great the next day. The body changes in subtle ways that only those that wear artificial limbs can imagine. (p.966)

If we substitute penis for limb in the above example, the crossover to trans men is clear. The statement below from an email newsletter about a new prosthetic called "the Bono" for trans men, titled "So yeah, I'll say it. I have penis envy" captures how the necessity for a penis is not just the territory of cis men.

> And yes, I'll admit I've always been fascinated by the penis. Ever since I knew such a thing existed, which is actually a very vivid memory. I would have been three. My brother was just born and I was watching my mother change his diapers, when I noticed something unusual between his legs. I asked my mother, "What is that?" to which she replied, "That's his penis," so I asked, "Well...why don't I have one of those?" to which my mother responded with, "Because you're not a boy." I remember thinking, thinking, thinking, obsessing and chewing on this for days. This was the moment I was first made acutely aware that I was in the eyes of the world, not a boy. And I remember thinking that it was kind of ridiculous that this tiny dangly appendage got to dictate so much. And I knew I really wanted one...
>
> And yes, in my sexual life, I've always felt there was something missing. I want to have sexual relationships with women, but I also want the presence of a penis. And I want it on me, not in me. Tricky...
>
> This is where the Bono is the closest thing I've ever found to giving me exactly that. A penis that feels a part of me. Something that I feel connected to and that stimulates me and my partner. In all honesty, I really couldn't imagine having to go without it now. But I guess that's how most men would feel about their penis, so really, there's probably nothing unusual about that at all. (Ben, June 17, 2017 email from ...Transthetics – Innovative Prosthetics for trans men et al...)

This person's experience seems to encapsulate the transition of a tool that is inert to one that is a *knowing* part of the body, i.e. something that is enveloped into what the body knows (De Preester & Tsakiris, 2009). De Preester and Tsakiris believe this is limited, but we have to push it to find space for trans people's lives to be livable, particularly when surgery is not always an option.

In the following extract, a cis man is talking about his experience with a prosthetic for his left foot which he was congenitally missing.

> One of the major factors in my satisfaction with a new prosthesis is how little I feel it. That may sound strange, but to me, my prosthesis is an extension of my body. (I can actually 'feel' some things that come into contact with it, without having to see them...). It must "feel" as close to not being there as possible. (Murray, 2004, p.970)

The presence of a phantom many times enables the individual to incorporate the prosthetic into their body matrix, which is relevant for those people with congenital absence of a limb and trans people. The interoceptive experience is the same across all these groups of people.

Sex with an(other) body

Being trans is not in and of itself an impairment that rises to the level of disability; the identity *is* subject to discrimination and minority stress. In considering sexual functioning for transgender people (with or without surgery/hormones), the threshold of impairment and disability is usually met. This is a physical impairment that may have psychological consequences. The following will dissect this intersection of sex with trans bodies.

Perceptions towards trans sex

There is a paternalism involved in sex in relation to disability and trans experience. Sex may not be seen as a necessary aspect of treatment or health in the disabled communities (Esmail *et al.*, 2010). In "Disabled Women Have Sexual Needs Too," Mitra Farazandeh (2017) clearly accounts for how perceptions of her disabled body made the possibility of her sexual needs invisible. She describes how she did not even see herself as human because of her physical deformity, so the recognition of her own need for love and desire was difficult to access.

This is analogous in trans communities where people may not believe that they deserve or have access to love and sex. As in the vaginoplasty example from earlier, trans women have been attempting to ask for a depth that works for them functionally and symbolically, and could be met by a surgeon who states that depth is unnecessary because a penis only needs a certain amount of depth to receive pleasure (Straayer, 2016). This demonstrates a few problematic assumptions. One, that sex is only for the pleasure of cis men. Two, that trans women only have sex with cis men. Three, that doctors should not listen to what patients need. If a trans woman feels that a deeper vaginal canal will improve her sex life, why not provide her with that? Maybe she enjoys large dildos with her girlfriend? Why would a surgeon argue this point unless it put the patient in danger? And lastly, that a woman's body-image in relation to her genitals has only to do with sex. Her genitals may have more to do with her identity or wearing a bathing suit than sex.

Partners

On the subject of partners, there is societal pressure for a disabled person to only seek other disabled people for sexual partners (Esmail *et al.*, 2010). This same pressure applies to trans people—trying to attract a cisgendered person would be shooting too high. There is an implicit bias that a cisgendered body/person is in a higher league than a trans body person. My trans patients who are dating almost always talk about this fear: "Who will want to be with me?" Even if it is a realistic bias/fear, it is not 100 percent true, so my job is to help encourage my patients to persevere; even if the pool of people is smaller, it does exist. Persons with disabilities face a similar insecurity that a partner without a disability could do better than a "defective" person (Esmail *et al.*, 2010). Both are seen as too complicated, burdensome and not worth the trouble.

There is also the stigma placed on people attracted to trans folks, as seen in this quote from a 30-year-old, multiracial trans woman in a 2017 study of internalized transphobia:

> If someone is actually attracted to us, then something is really wrong with that person. You can universally make a joke about a trans person, or having sex with a trans person, and the general public will think it's hysterical because we're viewed as fucking freaks. (Rood *et al.*, 2017, p.6)

Sexual attraction to trans people or disabled people is characterized as a fetish.

Another aspect of overlap between disability and trans is the belief that sex for pleasure is not an inherent right (Tepper, 2000). Historically, there has been an implicit bias that a trans person should want to pass visually but is being too demanding to want more than that. Furthermore, that if sex is a possibility, it should be enough to give the other pleasure. One should expect and not lament loss of sensation from top and bottom surgeries. Normality in sexuality has plagued bodies not seen as natural, either because of the effect of a disease or a perception that post gender-affirmative surgery bodies are "fake."

Trans/crip time

In disabilities studies, there is the concept of crip time. Crip time signifies the extra time someone needs to do an activity an able-bodied person can do in a shorter amount of time (Kafer, 2013). There is also a trans time, which includes some delays which occur during transition and the variable developmental trajectory, such as second puberty in middle-age, which I will tackle in the next chapter. Baril (2015) has combined these two concepts into trans/crip time, which he defines as the time it takes to research transition, heal from surgery, and the extra time at medical appointments getting your doctors up to speed on trans health. In our work here, let us think about trans/crip time in relation to the extra time needed to mentally, emotionally and physically prepare to have sex. For some trans feminine patients, the mental work to gear up for sex due to the lowering of their sex drive from hormones feels overwhelming and not worth the effort. There are some trans men who need to mentally conjure up their phantom penis throughout the sexual experience, which can be mentally exhausting, to try to mentally reduce the free energy from the incongruence of their anatomy (more about phantoms and how to use them later). Many of my trans patients who need a penile prosthetic to engage in sex, talk about the frustration of the time it takes to go strap it on and the mental setback involved. They explain how deflating to their sexual energy it is to have to take that pause to "put on their penis." It reminds them that they "don't have it" when they have to excuse themselves, undoing all the mental work they put into feeling connected to their penis. This is demonstrated in the following example:

> Specific sexual acts that enforce my lack of penis and presence of breast tissue bother me. I get frustrated that I can't fuck my partner the way I want (with the body parts I want). I am trying to work through some of this in therapy. (Hill-Meyer & Scarborough, 2014, pp.356–357)

Disabled bodies also must grapple with what can and cannot be done (or done without pain) during sex, with the accompanying mourning of lost sexual activity.

One trans patient recounted a conversation he had with his brother while they were on vacation. The brother had just hooked up with a woman and gotten a blow job. He was encouraging my patient to do the same, which was a positive moment of recognition of his masculinity but also a misunderstanding. My patient had to explain to him that first of all, he had not brought his penis with him, since his girlfriend did not come on this family vacation. Second, he could never have a spontaneous moment like that (even if he were single) since an explanatory conversation would have to happen first. This illustrates the impairment and disability split for this person. He was extremely relieved and satisfied to find the prosthetic accommodation worked so well, but it had its social limitations. The complications of explaining will be examined later in more detail.

This is in contrast to another patient who feels more dysphoric with a strap-on penis. He feels like it just reminds him he does not have a right-sized penis, particularly since he cannot feel sensation from it. He found that using his own body and finding ways for his own penis to touch his partner's body a better accommodation. This way he felt that it was his body in connection with his partner, without any mediator.

Sexual functioning

Reaching "normal" performance standards of the sexual response cycle is not in everyone's best interest. The Human Sexual Response Cycle was only defined using heterosexual cisgendered people as subjects (Masters & Johnson, 1966), the pathway being: excitement, plateau, orgasm to resolution. There is so much variety in sexual lives that the definition of sexual health using only this cycle is needlessly narrow.

A broader definition of sexual well-being takes into account how the individual experiences the intrapsychic and interpersonal aspects of their sexuality (Verschuren *et al.*, 2015). The focus shifts to a model where satisfaction may not include the full sexual response cycle but one could still feel fulfilled. We need to look at how we can use research on cis bodies and how it can be translated for trans bodies. For instance, the Nottingham Centre for Transgender Health has adjusted sex therapy interventions meant for cis women for trans women's bodies post-vaginoplasty (Robbins-Cherry, 2016). Their program challenges social/sexual norms, such as sex being only about penetration and points out how everyone's bodies look different. Then as part of the sexual growth program, the trans women practice at home, gaining control over vaginal muscles, doing vaginal mirror work, masturbating, and finally partner involvement and communication skills. There is also a need to improve sexual functioning for those who have not had genital surgery, which may actually be the majority of trans people.

Sexual dysfunction can be defined as impairment in sexual functioning coupled with distress, as opposed to sexual difficulty, which is impairment without distress (Elaut *et al.*, 2016). This European collaborative research group is following their trans patients through all forms of medical transition. They continue to find interesting data about the sexual lives of their patients with this ongoing research project (as yet unpublished).

One interesting finding is that initiation of sex for those who have not had surgery is a difficult hurdle across the gender spectrum. Post-bottom surgery, the ability to initiate for trans men vastly improves, from almost 35 percent difficulty to about 7 percent difficulty. For trans women, the change is negligible (Elaut *et al.*, 2016). Interpreting this finding, it seems to reveal that difficulty initiating sex may have more to do with dysphoria than desire. Other findings from this research included trans men's arousal difficulties reducing, their sexual desire increasing and pain during intercourse. For the trans women, their complaints were fairly similar.

Wierckx and colleagues (2004) studied trans mens' and trans women's responses to hormone treatment. Their research highlights the effect of hormones on our bodies and the need for adjustment for men and women. Their graph for sexual desire looks like steps ascending for trans men and steps equally descending for trans women. It speaks to the power of testosterone/estrogen on sexual desire and arousal. It also illustrates that the changes are not monolithic; and from my clinical experience, the shift in desire is not always wanted by the person. Some trans men are overwhelmed by the increase in sexual desire, while others love it but still need to adjust to it. For some trans women the dip in desire can be a relief but can complicate connection in a sexual relationship. How one defines sexual desire is also unique to the individual, as illustrated by the sex positive motto "Don't yuck my yum."

For some trans women, sexual arousal is more nuanced with hormonal changes, as other aspects of their body may have more stimulus reaction than their genitals. Julia Serano (2007) described how nipples were a larger source of pleasure after hormone treatment, which was a surprise to her. Or it is the alleviation of the body acting on its own as seen in this quote from *Trans Bodies, Trans Selves*: "It's very uncomfortable when this ugly thing which is unfortunately still between my legs 'wakes up again'" (Hill-Meyer & Scarborough, 2014). For trans men, however, increased blood flow and growth of clitoral tissue on testosterone may relocalize arousal to being primarily genital.

Van de Grift and colleagues (2016) questioned trans masculine people's sexual use of their body before and after testosterone was initiated. There was not much variability except less vaginal penetration post-T. Wierckx and colleagues (2011) asked trans men about their quality of life in relation to their body-image pre- and post-top surgery; there was improvement in their overall satisfaction with life and self-worth but none in connection to sufficiency as a sexual partner, pleasure in sexual activities or sufficiency as a man. Improved self-worth and life satisfaction are important aspects of self which contribute to sexual functioning but are more qualitative. If one feels more self-worth, it may make it easier to experiment sexually without feeling devastated if it does not work out. One's sense of self is less fragile, which allows for the flexibility to explore how bodily changes can be incorporated into one's sexual script or how one wants to rewrite it.

Visible versus invisible disabilities

The visible and invisible qualities in relation to sexual life are remarkably similar for people with disabilities and people of trans experience. Visible disabilities are primarily physical limitations which are apparent to the public, like walking with a cane or missing a limb. Invisible disabilities are those which are not outwardly recognizable, such as mental illness or visual impairment. Visible and invisible transness are defined by how well someone is perceived by others in their affirmed gender. Disclosure is the main concern related to visiblity/invisibility. The discourse around disclosure is quite similar for trans and disabled communities, particularly around whether one is "passing" as their affirmed gender or as a person without a disability. If, when and how to disclose is a recurrent clinical topic in session. The fears are similar in both communities, if you look at the following quotes from these research studies on disclosure: "I don't want to have to explain" (Esmail *et al.*, 2010. p.1153); "I am not sure whether to disclose, or when to disclose or what gets disclosed in the first place" (Esmail *et al.*, 2010, p.1153); "I usually don't consider myself disabled, except during sex" (Verschuren *et al.*, 2015, p.190). These could have easily been said by either a person with a disability or a trans person.

Shame is a major component of this reluctance to disclose. Disclosure can run up against self-image. One may feel that one's transgender history is so far in the past that it does not feel relevant to who one is now. It is also an aspect of trans/crip time, in that it takes time and energy away from an interaction. Disclosure also usually serves as a very unsexy thing to have to have a conversation about with a partner. There is no one way or timing to have this conversation. Some people prefer that prospective partners know up front even before meeting; they disclose on their online profile.

Trans/crip time is also applicable to the new aspect of sexual development in young people who have not had sex prior to transition and who may avoid sex until after surgery. The level of impairment for these young people is more profound in some ways. Even if you have had to experience sex in an incongruent body, it is hoped you had some experience asking for what you want from a partner, how your body reacts to different stimuli, etc. These experiences act as a point of reference when one becomes more embodied and likely more sexually active.

Questioning sex

Creativity requires limitations—the human struggle against limitations produces the creative act (May, 1975). Helping our patients feel empowered to name aspects of their body is a simple but profound intervention towards more present and satisfying sexual lives. What I have found is that it is not as important to have answers as a therapist as it is to know the right questions.

I have developed three realms of questioning categorized by senses in order to advance sexual functioning and well-being. The first is looking. What are the images my patient is looking at? If they are only looking at images of cisgender people having sex, then maybe I have to ask if they have ever seen porn with trans people engaged in sex (particularly porn produced by and for trans people in order to avoid fetishistic porn). If the only goal of sex is to have it like cis people, then it is setting oneself up for perpetual disappointment.

How does the patient's body look to their partner and to their own self during sex? Do they need a prosthetic or piece of clothing that aids in how they are seen? How do they keep their wig on, or other clothing or apparatus which is gender-affirming? Do they see their self differently depending on the gender of the partner(s)?

When language is utilized with power it is a form of action (Fischer, 2003). The following are questions which relate to listening and being heard or spoken about by others. Have they talked about what's different through social/medical transition and post-interventions with their partner(s)? The language we use to identify body parts cannot be underestimated. It is an act of owning one's body in an interactional, interpersonal manner. How does your patient want to hear their body talked about? What specific words do they want their body parts called? Can they ask for this? Is their partner able to mirror this? Is this something they can work on together or not? Ask each person to go through the body (not when they are expecting to have sex) and tell their partner what words feel good to call them or describe them.

Lastly, is the feeling in and of the body? How do they want to be touched? How do they want to be handled by a partner? How does one manage different body parts reaching one another or avoiding one another? Is there a fun way to do this? Does the partner feel comfortable touching or not touching certain areas? Is a once-prohibited area now accessible? How do they navigate if one partner's favorite activity is now off-limits? How do they communicate all this with multiple partners in a way that does not feel burdensome or bogged down? Do they need a prosthetic or sex toy that helps them engage in a sex act more aligned with their gender identity and expression? What are their fantasies? Can those be enacted? What feels different for them during sex depending on the gender of their partners? Do parts of their body feel different now? If they did/do sex work, how does sex feel different/the same with romantic partners?

One must be aware of the myriad options available to people as aids to sexual functioning: prosthetics (dildos, strap-ons), pumping, vibrators, masturbation sleeves, experimenting with sexual positions, visual aids and kink. The various sensations that can be accessed through different types of kink play can be less genital focused and thus possibly provoke less dysphoria and more inclusion. For example, there is a kink/sex party in New York City which has in its FAQ: "[We] are committed to creating an anti-oppressive space, to holding anti-white supremacist, anti-transmisogynist, anti-ableist, and consent-focused boundaries around the space that we create."[2] We must be audacious in our interventions in stretching patients to find safe ways to be creative in their sexuality.

It also cannot be emphasized enough that the brain is not just an "accessory to reproduction"; it is an essential sexual organ—not only for trans people but everyone; trans and disabled people just need to rely on it more (Jordan-Young, 2011). The mind needs to fill the gap between what the person desires and what the body can achieve.

Phantoms, the rubber hand illusion and its application to trans sex

The rubber hand illusion (RHI) is an interesting neurological phenomenon which illustrates how our mind remaps our body ownership. In this illusion, the person sits with one of their hands under a table, while a rubber hand is placed on the table where their actual hand would have been positioned. So, the person has their real left hand and the rubber right hand on the table. Then a different person synchronously touches the sitting person's right hand and rubber hand while the sitting person looks at the rubber right hand. Fairly quickly, the person will begin to "feel" the sensation in the rubber hand, and proprioceptive drift will occur making the person feel the position of their hand is the rubber hand. The illusion is a play on our vision, touch and proprioception. The multisensory experience of the RHI begins to update the priors to incorporate the rubber hand as part of "me" as opposed to "not me" because of the synchronous sensory input which combines the visual

---

2   www.mythpartynyc.com

and sensory information as a first-person experience as opposed to the rubber hand belonging to another person (Apps & Tsakiris, 2014). This multisensory experience includes all aspects of the body matrix including the peripersonal space (within 30 cm) within the visual field (Makin, Holmes & Ehrsson, 2008; Moseley *et al.*, 2011). It is the simplest explanation to the brain to adopt the rubber hand. It is also not only a viseo-tactile experience since the skin temperature of the person's real hand lowers when the person has incorporated the rubber hand, indicating full ownership of the rubber hand by the body (and pseudo dis-ownership of the real hand) proprioceptively and interoceptively (Moseley *et al.*, 2008). This cooling effect is believed to indicate changes in the body matrix due to shifts in neural activity (Moseley *et al.*, 2011).

People with higher IAcc perform worse on the RHI (Ainsley *et al.*, 2014; Tsakiris *et al.*, 2011). Researchers believe this is the case because people with higher IAcc have a greater ability to attend to their interoceptive signals and the fake hand does not have the priors signaling the brain, so the brain maintains its anchor to the real hand. The prediction errors will update the priors for the interoceptive signals in the real hand. It also suggests that in the absence of interoceptive signals, exteroceptive ones are privileged.

How can we capitalize on the plasticity of self-representation for the benefit of sexual functioning? Can we use the phenomena of RHI and phantoms to animate the prosthetics available? Prosthetics are tools which extend the body; we work to incorporate this tool into the body and the world (Leder, 1990). Not everyone can extend their body with a tool but may need to use the body they have in a new and creative way. For some, the tool is embodied as a means to body completion (De Preester & Tsakiris, 2009). With the help of a phantom and the prosthetic, can someone reach body completion? It is an important intervention to transform this mournful phantom sensation into something useful for the patient. For some trans men, their phantom penis breathes life into their prosthetic penis, but not every man will know that unless the therapist tells them of the possibility.

Then there is the possibility of incorporating someone else's penis as your own. For trans men who have sex with people with penises there can be a borrowing of the other's penis as his own. The power of this strategy is supported by the experience of leg amputees who experience itchiness in their phantom leg and who find relief in scratching the leg of another. It is a type of "tactile empathy" (Weeks & Tsao, 2010, p.464). This fits the theory that phantoms are a manifestation of the incompatibility of what is seen and what is felt.

The conundrum of genitals for trans men and trans women is inverse (for those dysphoric with the birth formation of them): building up as opposed to disappearing or displacing. Some trans women can create the visual erasure of their birth genitals by tucking, or can transpose anal sex into vaginal sex or orient herself to her penis as her clitoris. Free energy is reduced by the visual perception matching the emotional gender, just as it is reduced for trans masculine people with the visual aid of a prosthetic.

For some trans men, I believe we could apply the RHI. The visual of wearing a prosthetic can be helpful to reduce the prediction error of the expectation of seeing a penis, which reduces the mental noise. The RHI could be applied during masturbation or with a partner. The individual needs to be able to touch his own material penis while touching the prosthetic or have someone else touch his body and prosthetic (not everyone is comfortable with this so it already has a major limitation for some trans men). Synchronizing touch on the prosthetic penis and on his body, he may be able to provoke the remapping of his body and feel sensation in the prosthetic.[3] Some studies have shown that slow CT-optimal touch (the type of touch that activates c-fibers) works better in the RHI (Crucianelli *et al.*, 2013; Lloyd *et al.*, 2013; van Straleen *et al.*, 2014). Unfortunately, only the glans head of a penis has c-fibers, which is of no help to trans men (Cazala, Vienney & Stoléru, 2015). So, could the free nerve endings of the clitoris and vaginal mucosa be just as receptive to the RHI as c-fibers? We will need research to answer that for us.

The visual representation has to be as realistic as possible and in the right positioning (with the peripersonal space) since nondescript objects or ones in an unexpected placement usually do not produce the effect (Costantini & Haggard, 2007; Tsakiris & Haggard, 2005) but sometimes do (Armel & Ramachandran, 2003). Armel and Ramachandran were able to project sensation to a table instead of the rubber hand, proving it is possible to transfer sensation. There can be interoceptive and proprioceptive transference in this illusion. The results of Tsakiris and Haggard's (2005) study suggest that the RHI reflects the top-down influence of body integration. This is optimistic for the application of the RHI for trans people, since gendered predictions and multisensory information contribute to body ownership. Utilizing and learning with a body part increases its representation in the cortex (Nude *et al.*, 1996; Recanzone *et al.*, 1992). Can we harness all of this to improve sexual functioning? Schafer and colleagues (2007) were able to provoke feeling in an artificial third arm visually connected to the subjects in between their two arms. So why couldn't we induce sensation in a body part the subject already feels from internal sensory prediction? Amputees were also taught how to move their phantom

---

3   We need to do control group research studies to know what variables allow the RHI to work (i.e. higher/lower IAcc, phantom/no phantom, type of touch, type of prosthetic, self/other touch, etc.).

to transform their wrist into feeling as if it was a wheel or axis-type joint (Moseley & Brugger, 2009).

Even if the full RHI effect does not happen, there may still be the secondary benefit of the visual congruence in both solo or partner attempts at sexual fulfillment, since the mental work of visualizing the body is not there. Additionally, during masturbation, the tactile reinforcement from the hand on the prosthetic may be beneficial. These actions can still reduce prediction error and thus there is less mental friction leading to a freer mind to enjoy.

Shame

It may not be a coincidence that in some languages (German, Greek, Danish) the word shame is derived from the word for genitalia (Zahavi, 2014). We collectively and culturally have a complicated relationship to sexual organs. Drawing from Young's formulation of oppression (2011) we can orient the directions from which shame induction attacks the individual. They are exploitation, marginalization, powerlessness, cultural domination and violence. These are the fronts that can be at play when we are working to filter shame.

To be able to employ any of these sexual accommodations may take some process of working through shame first. How do we begin? We need to reject cisnormative ideas about sexuality or what Wilkerson (2012, p.183) calls "normate sex." If trans people are to feel positive about their sexual lives, then they cannot be measured against people with different bodies. Wilkerson bonds the non-normative sexualities of trans and disabled bodies as highlighting the social category of disability. As with folks with disabilities who need to free themselves from "normal penetrative sex," so too do trans folks (Esmail *et al.*, 2010, p.1152). One freedom disabled people have found is upending the phases of sex acts (Siebers, 2012). Sex does not need to follow the Masters and Johnson beginning, middle and end of the sexual response cycle. Siebers goes on to say that disabled folks (trans folks) need to think expansively about how they define what is sexual. If classical erogenous zones are not sensitive, then expand the map to other areas of the body.

The use of tools (for gender and/or sexual expression) can be veiled with shame. If I can, I reframe these tools for a patient, as not some extra apparatus, but as something that Stiegler (1998) argues is an extension of being human. Heidegger (1927) argued that the use of tools are an essential part of humanity and culture. It is about extending one's body map to include whatever tool will be necessary. Many patients have internalized the transphobic misconception that tools are "not real" or "faking it." Dislodging this myth is a substantial role the therapist needs to play. Knowing about and encouraging the use of any tools that contribute to reducing the free energy is a useful tack. The boundaries of what is human are flexible and penetrable; tools can be incorporated into their limits (De Preester & Tsakiris, 2009). The tool becomes incorporated into the body matrix, like Merleau-Ponty's (1945/1962) example of a cane for the visually impaired.

A study of men with disorders of sex development in sexually satisfying relationships found that they had discovered ways to reach orgasm outside of intercourse and to satisfy partners' needs alternatively as well (Van Seters & Slob, 1988). It is incumbent on therapists to support the discovery of what is possible through experimentation, pornography, classes, websites, or by any means necessary. If trans people *only* try to recreate cisnormative sex, then there will always be a level of disappointment.

Mental distraction is a major culprit in unraveling a sexual experience. The mental work trans people already need to do in order to get aroused, stay aroused, embody themselves and visualize their bodies differently are tools towards satisfaction, but also serve as a distraction. Distraction is a major barrier to sexual functioning, as found in studies of cis men with erectile dysfunction. Researchers have found that unconscious and conscious distraction related to anxiety and worry about performance undermined sexual response and recognition of sexual cues, even when no physical dysfunction was present (Barlow, 1986; Janssen & Everaerd, 1993).

There are two types of distraction: inhibition and interference. Inhibition is suppression of intrusive thoughts such as memories, which we will talk more about in connection with trauma in the next chapter. Interference is when multiple stimuli struggle for attention in the individual (Harnishfeger, 1995; Janssen & Bancroft, 2006). This is a top-down and bottom-up process. Top-down is interference from within the individual mediated by the frontal lobe, whereas bottom-up is intruding from outside stimuli mediated by the amygdala (Compton, 2003; de Jong, 2009). Frontal regions can have a reciprocal effect on amygdala regions, thus attentional processes are a major component to the emotional process of sexual arousal (de Jong, 2009). Additionally, we know that cis men and cis women can use their minds to increase and diminish sexual arousal through fantasies or unpleasant thoughts (Cerny, 1978; Laws & Rubin, 1969). One study of cis men who were sexually functional found that they used attentional focus to stay connected to erotic stimuli whereas dysfunctional cis men focused on non-sexual signals, each creating their own feedback loop, either positive or negative (Wiegel, Scepkowski & Barlow, 2007).

Distraction caused by negative thoughts leads more to sexual dysfunction than anxiety itself (Barlow, 1986). There are no studies on trans men and women with this specificity, but I think we can extrapolate from these studies the importance of the mind as a sexual organ. It may be the best defense against internalized shame and the negative thoughts that infiltrate the mind.

We should also keep in mind that this process is heavily reliant on flexibility, working memory, inhibition, interference control, and other executive functions which are usually found to be at a deficit in people with autism spectrum disorder (ASD; Sinzig *et al.*, 2008). Since there is a higher percentage of ASD within the trans community than in the general population, this may make sexuality doubly complicated (Janssen, Huang & Duncan, 2016). Poor eye contact alone can preclude one from effective flirting. As therapists, we need to keep in mind that multiple, layered experience affects sex and relationships, which may or may not have to do with being transgender.

Autistic children have a deficit in their precision of interoceptive prediction errors. This has two effects. One is that the infant will be hypersensitive to interoceptive cues. Second, this hypersensitivity affects the ability to sense the self from others, which means that, if we think about bonding during breastfeeding, the infant cannot learn that the (m)other is the nurturing and prosocial object (Quattrocki & Friston, 2014). These and other sensory processing difficulties should be in our awareness when working on touch and sexual issues with these patients in therapy.

According to Janssen & Bancroft (2006) "the interface between psychological processes and genital response thus seems to depend heavily on two factors: the presence of a sexual stimulus, and the absence of processes interfering with the activation of a response to a sexual stimulus" (p.198). This means the more one can reduce signal to noise ratio (lower free energy), the clearer the path is for sexual stimuli. The less static, the better able one is to be connected to and relax into a sexual experience.

Clinically, we need to keep in mind how attachment styles can impact sexual functioning. There are working memory deficits for both positive and negative attachment related information for avoidantly attached people and there will be inhibition in processing information that is perceived as distressing (Edelstein, 2006). As we saw in Chapter 3, our trans patients may be more likely to develop an avoidant attachment style.

Acceptance

The importance of accepting one's trans identity cannot be overstated for its protective factors when it comes to overcoming shame (Bockting, Robinson & Rosser, 1998). Acceptance of the body as an imperfect project is an important clinical goal (Langer, 2014). Only through working through shame and internalized transphobia can a person know what they want and allow themselves to ask for it. This also applies to the partners of trans people and people with disabilities. In both these groups, partners are seen in three ways: as fetishists if they are attracted to nonconforming bodies; or that they must be uncomfortable with their partner's body; or that they are making a sacrifice to be with the trans/disabled person. For all involved, we need to dispel these myths and see all sex as deviant so that no one's sex is deviant.

There is also the need to work though shame and fear of what it means for the individual to have sex in the manner of their fantasies. Is there fear for the trans man that if he enjoys receiving vaginal penetration it means he isn't really a man? Or is the trans woman undermining her ability to transpose anal sex for vaginal sex as "not a real" experience? Positive sexual schemas result in more sexual response and pleasure (this was found in cis women; Janssen *et al.*, 2000). These include viewing sex as pleasurable, important, and one's body as being able to respond sexually (i.e. seeing oneself as a sexual being). Positive sexual schemas may be difficult to imagine for someone struggling with shame, especially when most images of sex are with cis, able-bodied people. Finding or creating new schemas can be an empowering exercise towards reclaiming a positive sexual life.

The point to be reinforced here is that we (i.e. clinicians and community) need to be creative. Clinicians cannot help patients if we do not recognize the impairment that does come with being trans. It *is* physically impossible for many trans people to have sex in an ego-syntonic manner. Even for those whose bodies are congruent, there are still periods of learning and adjustment towards full sexual functioning. Accommodating for bodies is a comradeship and we should be open to how we can help each other. Coalition (trans/disabled/therapist/patient) is always a better stance than standing on distinctions.

CHAPTER 6

Trauma, Trans and Temporality

This chapter on trauma is divided into two parts: the first part will concern itself with the trauma of trans time within a developmental framework, the latter will address the intersections of gender trauma and other forms of emotional and bodily trauma in clinical work. The trans time traumas can be characterized as small "t" traumas, whereas gender trauma and the other traumas discussed in the second part are big "T" traumas. These are differentiated between smaller adverse experiences (small "t"), which would not reach the clinical level of an acute trauma but cumulatively create pressure on one's mental health, and big "T" traumas, which are the usual events (rape, sexual abuse, physical abuse, torture, verbal abuse, etc.) we associate with trauma reactions (Shapiro, 2001). The chapter will interrogate the traumas that are unique to being trans and how the recovery from other big "T" traumas may be complicated in trans embodiment. Transgender people appear to be exposed to potentially big "T" traumatic events at higher rates, possibly as high as twice as likely, than cisgender men and women, particularly if they are presenting in their affirmed gender (Shipherd *et al.*, 2011). Of a sample of Dominican transgender women with suicidality, the rates of severe trauma were startling: 23.9 percent experienced sexual abuse, 33.0 percent experienced psychological abuse, 12.3 percent were tortured, and 20.3 percent experienced a murder attempt (Budhwani *et al.*, 2018).

Clearly, gender specialists also need to be trauma specialists, and trauma specialists need to be gender specialists. Therefore, I have devoted this chapter to a variety of traumas. The purpose is to develop a frame of reference for clinicians to ask better questions in treatment so patients can connect better to their embodied selves to process these traumas.

Part one: Trauma of trans time

This book places gender at the core of the self as an element as fundamental as one's sense of humanness. How and when the subject accesses this foundational aspect of their consciousness can be convoluted and is in the subject's own time. I will begin with a discussion of the distinct qualities of the trans temporalities.

The philosopher Sydney Shoemaker (2011) talks about thin and thick properties of human existence, being changeable and stable, respectively. Neo-Lockean theory says that psychological properties are thick and the body consists of thin ones. Persistence of personhood consists of psychological continuity. How do we know any aspect of our selves? We know our selves because we persist through time in our memory and consciousness. We are first subjects of mental properties and second, but essentially, of physical properties according to Shoemaker (2011).

If we think about the Soul of the Prince thought experiment, it is particularly relevant to trans experience. The brain (specifically the cerebrum) of a prince is transplanted into the body of a cobbler. We can conclude that the personality, the humanness of the prince will go with the cerebrum, and the cobbler is lost. The subjectivity of the prince prevails, thus psychology over biology. Trans experience reinforces this conclusion to a degree. The conditional aspect is that we know the body has a reciprocal relationship with the mind. Trans people experience this (interoceptively and exteroceptively) prior to social, prosthetic or medical interventions but acutely, clearly, after a needed gender-affirming intervention when the individual feels the alignment. In addition, the subtle effects hormones have on our personalities reveal the high level of reciprocity happening within the human system such as is shown in the MMPI studies. Yet the core of the personhood lies in the mental states; biology can lean on those states but does not override it.

Shoemaker defines existence as "temporal parts of human animals, that we are bundles of mental states and events" (2011, p.352). He goes on to explain that mental states leave memories over and through time. We cannot think of ourselves without the temporal. Even though time is a function of the self [$t=f(\text{self})$], there is not an organ dedicated to its perception (Wittmann, 2009). We have dedicated organs for all other types of perception—eyes, ears, skin, etc. Wittmann considers time as one attribute of the self.

The experience of time is elastic and relative. It is not some objective phenomenon but is subject to one's emotions (Einstein, 1961; Geoffard & Luchini, 2010). It is not a thing that happens outside the self. Time is endogenous through indexing emotional states moment to moment (Craig, 2009b). Emotions register in two ways: physiologically and affective valence (affective valence being how positive or negative it is; Geoffard & Luchini, 2010). So, if one is anticipating a positive experience, one will be more aware of the passage of time (Fraisse, 1984). Furthermore, the experience of that time will feel like more time has passed, whereas the opposite will happen when it is a dreaded event—time will contract (Geoffard & Luchini, 2010). Time accelerates when we are doing something pleasurable; it drags during boredom and can be distorted during a traumatic event (Hancock & Weaver, 2005; Wittman, 2009). For instance, during a state of fear our mind is hyperaware and can record more memories during a short duration, which makes one feel as if the trauma lasted longer than the "actual" time it took.

Our body-image never really ages with us; we see ourselves usually as a younger version (Critchley, 1979)—in some ways, not old but not too young either. We normalize ourselves in our internal self-image. A friend of mine recently joked that he has dreams sometimes where he still has all his hair. And a colleague told me about her patient who was dreaming of himself in his affirmed gender now that he has accepted transition is right for him.

Those with a higher interoceptive awareness also have a greater awareness of the passage of time, further emphasizing the subjective nature of time (Craig, 2015). Subjective perception and interoception are beginning to make a basis for a new neural theory of time: that more awareness of your bodily and emotional life could lead to an extension of subjective perception of length of time (Wittmann, 2009). Wittmann goes on to equate "the flow of time" and "the flow of interoceptive signaling," both of which register in the dorsal posterior insula (p.1962).

In the history of trans, time was a primary factor in gaining access to treatment. If a person approached a doctor for care, the first question was usually "How long have you felt like this?" or "How long have you lived like this?" There was/is a misunderstanding that time equals legitimacy. The construction of knowledge "depends on the ability to map what happens over time" (Damasio, 1999, p.189). However, the construction of knowledge about gender has its own sense of timing, like anything long suppressed and repressed. This is why I argue against the poor terms in psychiatry of "early and late onset" when referring to gender dysphoria, as opposed to early and late awareness. The years or months a person needs to know their true self and even know what is possible is determined by many factors argued in this book as well as including access to internet, trauma history (which can sever the subject's ability to connect to their core feelings), fear of loss of loved ones, societal prejudice, and many others (Langer, 2016). In clinical meetings and conferences, I have heard professionals question the legitimacy of a trans person's identity because they came to it in later life, "convincingly" played the part of their gender assigned at birth or were "too" gender fluid ("they should just make up their mind already"). Paradoxically, clinicians/researchers then also characterize certainty and demand for access to treatment *now* as perseverative, obsessive, rigid, impatient or having poor impulse control (Zucker *et al.*, 2017) even though, in all children, gender-related interest is described as rigid as a part of normal child development (Martin & Ruble, 2004).

These notions of time are relevant to trans experience since the process of transition is characterized by waiting, anticipating, longing and urgency. What some therapists mistake for impatience in their trans patients in accessing interventions (I hear this from supervisees and colleagues new to working with trans patients) is just the fact that no one would want to wait to be their whole self. For the trans person whose repressed gendered feelings have all been freed and the solution understood, enduring the wait (due to medical access waiting lists, relationship negotiation, time off work, etc.) is a painful reality. Many people are traumatized by the wait, mostly in a small "t" trauma level, but this could rise to a more severe level depending on the individual's psychic structure and coping skills. The mental anguish in that limbo is possibly the most frustrating to work with in psychotherapy, since we know that the real, sustained relief will occur when the intervention is carried out. The usual compromises and accommodations cease to work for the individual. One patient of mine who decided to have phalloplasty after many years of feeling "OK enough" without it, felt intense pressure and impatience for when surgery would happen once he came to the insight that he needed it. This impatience took him by surprise since he has been living as a man for many years without anguish. Furthermore, the accommodations he had made around sex became dissatisfying in this interim period.

What can ameliorate this distress? Validating the distress and unfairness of the situation is sometimes all one can offer; also, supporting the thoughts or actions which provide some relief, like dressing, a favorite sport or reading. Many times, in treatment, once someone has a date (for hormones, surgery, transitioning at work, etc.) there can also be some relief in just knowing there is an end point on the horizon. Ambiguity is usually the worst since knowing one can or cannot have surgery for instance allows one to just accept the reality rather than living in limbo.

There is the amplification of time during recovery from surgery as another example of trans time which can feel traumatic. When one is in pain there is the danger of despair using the weapons of transphobic insults of others on the self: "What have I done?" "Why have I subjected myself to this?" "I've mutilated myself." "I'm a monster." It is a delicate clinical moment to help a patient contain this desperation while they have drains, wound vacs, pain and possible complications (hematomas, fistulas, infections and pain). Psychotherapy is usually a place for developing tolerance for ambiguity, but at those moments—certainly at least until acute injury is healed—it is what is needed for containment. Even for the most physically and mentally healthy person, surgery is a trauma. There are two phases to recovery, particularly in gender-affirming surgeries: being out of acute physical harm and aesthetic/functional completion. Even with a smooth recovery, questions linger: "How am I really going to look?" "How will I function?" These are practical and yet existential questions.

The truncating and elongating of time through various medical interventions can manifest itself in a myriad of ways for the subject. If one is to have surgery, one's life becomes suspended for two to six weeks or longer depending on the procedure. When is the right timing for such an interruption? Eventually one will return to the freedom to just *being* again post-intervention.

Some people accessing hormones or waiting for surgery keep themselves home until they "see a change" in their appearance. This self-imposed confinement is based on fear, shame or other difficult circumstances. One patient of mine did not want to start college until she "could pass," which kept her in more difficult financial and social circumstances, delaying the start of her career.

Trans time can mean slower time when one is still concerned about "passing." This can be in subtle ways such as getting ready and dressed in the morning; there are all the micro decisions that need to be made in order to solve the algorithm of gender expression. As illustrated in Chapter 5, the extra time needed in order to prepare for and have sex is in its own time. There is time lost in contemplating which bathroom to use to affirm one's gender but to avoid harassment, or the travel time to the floor with the gender-neutral restroom in one's office building, or running to the coffee shop on the corner to use the bathroom there instead of the one used by co-workers.

Time slippage is in some way no more apparent than with youth who are commencing hormone blockers. These kids are suspending their biological development while psychosocially they are continuing their development. What gets lost? How differently will this pre-teen be treated when they look so much younger than their age? Children, families and providers must weigh up multiple factors when deciding to start affirmative hormone treatment. Obviously, the alternative of not suspending an unwanted puberty is not a viable option, but we cannot underestimate this alternative form of incongruence and must be sensitive to it.[1] This is also a moment, due to this delay, when the first visibility of transness appears for this youth. It may also be the last, since once affirmative hormone treatment begins, physically the teen can "catch up" to their peers.

With children and adolescents, hormone intervention and development are particularly acute when it comes to fertility and sex. For example: for some people the urgency to transition removed their ability to have their own biological children, having not paused to freeze sperm or eggs (or not having had the finances to do it); or the young trans man who feels very positive about his ability to live stealth, except he is attracted to women and needs to mourn that he cannot biologically impregnate his partner; or the trans girl who will not be able to carry her own children. Some younger patients I have seen can find acceptance in family planning alternatives, just as I have seen cis patients who were infertile go through a similar process.

In the sexual realm, when bottom surgery does not feel like, or is not, a viable option, there is the same mourning

---

1   For more in-depth literature on gender diverse youth, see work written by Diane Ehernsaft, Michelle Angelo, Elijah Nealy, Arlene Istar-Lev and Irwin Krieger.

and creative process and "catching up" in learning and experience. How do I have sex in a way that is closest to what my mind and body expect? Since some people avoid sex because it provokes their dysphoria, they lose that time to experiment. This avoidance may impact their ability to learn how to have fulfilling sex post-bottom surgery. If one has not learned what feels satisfying sexually before, it may take longer to learn it with reconstructed anatomy.

I want to be clear that these are points of clinical consideration to have in mind to explore with individuals and families and should not be used as a means to control or deny access to care. Life is complicated and in any major decision something is always gained or lost. My position as a clinician is to create the space to clearly investigate all those options.

There is also the immediacy of the change (which is positive), which then opens up the depths of the misgendering trauma, interpersonally and internally. For instance, a trans woman's leftover fear of "exposure" changing in the women's locker room post-vaginoplasty is a kind of traumatic hypervigilance which is no longer necessary. Post-intervention(s) is where residual stress related to gender, behavior and the body require working through to come to terms with and accept the new reality. The internal, interoceptive felt trauma will be discussed later in this chapter.

Developmental stages or the timing of being an adult
This section will take certain developmental phases and explore how they have been addressed in clinical practice. Developmental stages are temporal by nature: the psychologist matches chronological age with developmental age. The developmental process for transgender individuals who begin to live their authentic gender in

adulthood has a wider slippage of time which can provoke a kind of small "t" trauma in contrast to those who recognize their gender earlier in life. Each has their own challenges and rewards.

I will be using the Erikson stages of human development, even though his descriptions of these stages are quite hetero/cis-normative. I believe this is justified because there is still merit and universality in the progression of each stage, even if I disagree with the specific goals Erikson uses as examples. These struggles and milestones are present in daily clinical work. How one accomplishes the tasks of each stage will be seen through a more diverse and post-modern lens.

First, let us look at those people who transition as adults who must travel through a second puberty, long after their first. Erikson's (1963) identity versus role confusion is the primary venture of adolescence where everything prior is up for re-examination. In the realm of gender, a trans person can be stalled in this stage or struggle with earlier developmental tasks. This confusion could cloud one's identity development in subtle and obvious ways. For instance, imagine the burgeoning trans man, coming of age in the 1960s, who declines a college scholarship for teaching because he would have to wear skirts and dresses in his professional career. This decision may or may not be made consciously considering gender, but is surely affected by it. He may then begin to think of himself as not smart or academic and apply for jobs below his skill level. If he then begins to live his authentic gender later in life, he will have to come to terms with the career path that was lost and the identity he developed because of it.

The other adjustment is how does one live in one's affirmed gender when one may not understand or know all the nuanced socializations that are taught in childhood and adolescence? This could lead to role confusion.

For instance, if a person is being seen as a man, he cannot compliment women on their appearance the same way he did when he was read as female. If he does not realize this, he could be confused by their reactions; and if it is at a workplace, it could be read as sexual harassment.

There is almost no one who feels that they transitioned early enough. Experientially, it may place one in Erikson's (1963) initiative versus guilt. Why did I not take the chance to transition sooner? There is a re-evaluation of time and timing: What is left of my lifetime? Without a boyhood or girlhood, an adolescence or even a young adulthood in my affirmed gender, which of those experiences are still possible? How can I appropriately capture developmental milestones from moments beyond my age? Resolution can mean taking solace in the initiative one is taking now as opposed to stagnating in the guilt.

There is the moment in time when one must accept what is lost. A reverberation of transition in the temporal arena is the loss of time. Just as trans people are faced with mourning and accepting their bodies as imperfect projects, so too they must confront the lost time (Langer, 2014). In my practice, I have seen that this confrontation happens once the initial joy of living more authentically fades into everyday banality. There is the recognition of what was missed, and what one can do with time left. The individual needs to be able to recognize and mourn for this lost time, be that physical or metaphorical. However, these moments have echoes of Erikson's (1963) autonomy versus shame and doubt, an earlier more primary stage. He characterizes this stage as the simultaneous tasks of "holding on and letting go" (p.251). Overcoming shame is a primary task through transition, where the ultimate achievement is autonomy of self. What do I try to attain (with medical, social, legal interventions) or reclaim, and what do I need to accept and move on? The developmental danger of this stage is obsessive regulation in an effort to hold onto control. I have seen this dynamic play out in trans folks who attempt to have complete control over their appearance, in body and behavior, to be perfect: perfectionism as a defense against shame.

Oli Rodriguez is a visual artist who created a video art project that illustrates healthy reclamation and acceptance. Rodriquez transitioned in his early adulthood, so never had a "boyhood." He never learned to play baseball, so he signed himself up for a pre-adolescent baseball clinic. Being early in transition, he looked much younger than his actual age and thus blended in with the other boys. There is a split-screen where on one side the video comprises images of him being taught baseball fundamentals, with the other boys with voice-over of him and his mother talking about his participation; the other side is a re-enactment of the baseball clinic by gender-ambiguous adults. In his words:

> The Baseball Project visualizes my immersion as a 26-year-old into a baseball clinic for 8–12 year old boys. The narration by my mother alters the gaze of the piece, directing the audience to examine my validity. An additional layer involves the redoing of the performance with gender-ambiguous adults. I contemporarily embody an adult role as a trans queer man and a child role as a 12-year-old. This functions on a personal level to redo a "male" childhood, and also engages the performance of gender and consent as a construct. (Rodriguez, 2008)

His ability to pass as a pre-adolescent boy was advantageous at the time, but in other circumstances it can be a liability (more on that later). The video is a simple but creative sublimation. The project embodies multiple layers; the creative reconstruction to reclaim his lost time. This loss is acquired in a shortened time frame. It allows intersubjective understanding through the gaze and commentary of his mother—to be seen, mirrored and recognized. It is a kind of triple mirroring—the video of himself, the mother's gaze and the re-enactment by the "gender-ambiguous adults." The need to create art has persisted through evolution because it has served a life-regulating function, not just as social communication (Damasio, 2010). Creative acts return one to the state of general well-being.

The other aspect that Rodriquez's work reveals is being seen as younger than your age as a trans man during—and, for some, for many years after transition—however, the opposite may be the case for some trans women. The way one is treated can be determined by others assuming one's age. This can range from the benign (a new friend assumes you've not seen a certain culturally relevant movie) to the detrimental (not being taken seriously at a job interview because the interviewer assumes you are much younger or older than you are).

Trans people have access to perspectives on age and gender that others cannot experience. As uncomfortable or even embarrassing as it could be to go through puberty again in middle age for instance, how many people get a do-over in life? To go through this extraordinary change with the knowledge and insight of adulthood is not something most people will ever experience in their lifetime. And isn't the definition of a life fully lived one that provides us with new perspectives?

The suspended or regressed time during a medical transition is a unique experience of the self in time and space. These shifts in time can be exhilarating but bring their own type of dissonance. The relativity of time presses on our psyches and we will bend at our most vulnerable places. Despite all this time slippage, the thick properties of the self will prevail. Erikson (1963) warns us that despair will overcome ego integrity if we feel time is too short to start living as we wish. If there is one thing trans people know more profoundly than anyone, it is that it is never too late to live as your self.

Part Two: Intersections of traumas and gender trauma

According to Bromberg, the therapeutic "relationship is an interpersonal environment that frees patients' potential and appetite for a creative dialectic between their internal reality and the presentation of external reality as represented by the analyst as an independent center of subjectivity" (1998, p.4).

It has been my experience from patients' accounts and in professional meetings that the trauma (big "T" traumas such as rape, assault, childhood sexual, emotional or physical abuse) a trans person has experienced can be misunderstood as etiological of their trans identity or gender expression. This fundamental misreading is dangerous. It is dangerous for many reasons, but primarily because pathologizing gender forecloses any honest and safe exploration of one's gender and one's trauma. Of course, a person's expression is shaped by trauma, such as how one presents within one's gender expression (as more modest or more revealing) after child sexual abuse, but one's core gender identity does not change.

What we foundationally offer our patients is a time and place where they can freely and safely be their whole self; anything that interrupts this is anti-therapeutic. We can recognize that the trauma has surely shaped the individual in some way, but to pathologize their gender identity or expression is a manipulation of one's position as therapist and only serves to install shame.

We maintain the scene in which the patient can experience and find the self. "Me-ness" is constituted from the reflection from the other. As discussed earlier in the book, TGNC children are reflected a gendered "me-ness" that reinforces a sense of gender misalignment with the child's own internal signals of their gender. It is incumbent upon therapists to be genuinely mirroring their trans patients, to practice embodied mentalization, as this will facilitate further embodiment for the patient.

One understanding of trauma is of the subject losing their sense of time. One is traumatized by something in one's history because the brain does not allow one to think and react to it as a past event, but instead behaves as if it is still happening. The subject is stuck in the moment of the trauma. Time is an anchoring criterion of diagnosing trauma. If a patient is hypervigilant in the moment of the crisis, that is adaptive, but if they are still hypervigilant nine months later, it is maladaptive and therefore trauma. They have not been able to regulate on their own.

We also know that our bodies are where our trauma is stored (Haines, 2015; van der Kolk, 2015). The experience and memory of trauma is embodied. It is an interoceptive event. In order for healing to occur, we need to enlist the body in the treatment. We do this through asking questions about the state of the body in the moment or through Eye Movement Desensitization and Reprocessing (EMDR) or creative arts therapy. In the same way that we cannot think our way into gender, one cannot rely only on the mind in relation to trauma.

Paulus & Stein (2010, p.458) propose the term "interoceptive prediction schemas" to describe the mental construction that occurs when the individual interprets their interoceptive afferent signals. How this relates to trauma is that those people who have experienced repeated traumas will have to work harder to modulate their negative predictions of their bodily signals that something bad is happening. If I am recovering from a cardiac arrest, whenever I feel sensations in my chest, I may interpret them as another arrest even though they are benign sensations. The other reason is that when one is dissociated from one's body, one can no longer feel the body one is inhabiting. This is a common occurrence in the case of trauma.

Trauma does not relent to time. It does not respect time, in that the trauma is formed by it staying in the present of the individual's mind/body even though the external event has passed. It is this anchor in time of the evolutionary response to threat with fight, flight or freeze which haunts the individual. Evolution did not just provide us with fight, flight or freeze, otherwise we would not seek out contact with others. We were also endowed with an attachment system that provides for a "push–pull" type of motivation towards social interaction (Porges, 2003). And as could be expected, how these are mediated is dependent on one's attachment style. If social interactions go well, it counterbalances the instinct to fear others. There are two moments where this is relevant to gender: there is the internal trauma of living incongruently prior to needed social and medical interventions; then there is the hypervigilance in social situations of being misgendered by others.

The shape and impact of gender trauma

Trauma and trans are beginning to be discussed and researched, but the work conspicuously leaves out the nature of the trauma of subjectively experiencing incongruent aspects of the body on a minute-by-minute basis. There is preliminary research about the diverse and specific ways the trans communities can be traumatized across the lifespan as well as before, during and after transition (Ainsworth & Spiegel, 2010; Budge, Adelson & Howard, 2013; Burnes *et al.*, 2016; dickey *et al.*, 2017; Herman, 2013). Burnes and colleagues (2016) isolated common areas of traumatization for transgender people. It begins with traumas within the family of origin, intrapersonal (self-harm) trauma, interpersonal violence during transition (social and medical) and public bathroom trauma which can be seen across the above-mentioned studies. These are traumas committed on the surface of the body. For instance, a trans woman experiencing more or less harassment pre- or post-facial feminization surgery is interactional and exteroceptive (seeing herself in the mirror); it is not about interoception. What I will explore here is the intrapsychic and interoceptive trauma perpetrated by the body on the self. The emotional and physical anguish the subject can endure at various levels before, during and after needed interventions and how other traumas complicate the clinical picture. It cannot be stated enough that this is not the case for everyone—the quality of experience is a spectrum as well as the gender, but that gender trauma can be seen as a big "T" or small "t" trauma, depending on the person.

Gender trauma could be defined as the profound and consistent disruption of the self by the mis-attunement of the body and society. In addition, gender trauma includes the emotional burden bearing upon the individual's psyche due to the internal dissonance, the overwhelming allostatic load of gendered free energy. This trauma de-facilitates the trans individual's ability to connect with their own body and other people, due to alienation from the body and possibly from attempting to act in an incongruent gender role. I am expanding on Saketopoulou's (2014) "massive gender trauma," which she defines as the trauma of living in an incongruent gender. This burden can be unbearable, particularly for the most psychically fragile people. Through a child case, Saketopoulou demonstrates how one can develop a psychotic defensive reaction to living in gender incongruence. She underlines that being trans is not the psychotic formation, but the psychotic reaction may develop under the pressure surrounding identifying as a gender other than the one assigned at birth. If the gender trauma is not addressed early, the psychotic compromise can become ensconced, which is why psychotherapy with a skillful therapist is imperative. If the therapist would pathologize the trans identity, it would have extremely detrimental effects on the child's mental health.

When "the other systematically 'disconfirms'" the subject's state of mind, particularly in strong affective states, the individual "mistrusts" their own sense of the self and reality. Dissociation becomes the "most adaptive solution to preserving self-continuity" (Bromberg, 1998, p.11; Laing, 1962). One may feel inhuman or even be explicitly called an "it" (Burnes *et al.*, 2016). The individual's ability to cope with this dislocation is dependent on their personality structure. In Saketopoulou's (2014) child patient, the psyche was vulnerable to psychotic processes and under the stress of gender incongruence was further compromised. Remarkably, her work with Saketopoulou appears to have protected her from developing a full psychosis.

The following quote from a trans man illustrates the path to dissociation: "When I reached puberty, reality took hold when my period started. What was happening to my body felt so unnatural. I was horrified and dissociated with every part of my body from the neck down" (Henry, 2017, p.107). One study found dissociation was higher (derealization, depersonalization and absorption) in trans people compared to non-clinical samples of cis participants, but lower than those diagnosed with Dissociative Identity

Disorder (Kersting *et al.*, 2003). This higher score is skewed when using the Dissociative Experiences Scale (DES) by a question that trans people will likely highly endorse which asks about feeling unable to recognize one's body. Even if we correct for this question, in the Kersting study sample, trans participants still had elevated, clinical threshold scores. The DES is widely used as part of the assessment for EMDR treatment. Kersting and colleagues caution that it may not be as valid when working with trans patients. I believe this also depends on where in a person's gender quotient they are at the time you administer the scale. I have had patients who have said that they would have endorsed that item much more highly pre-transition and others who still endorse it relatively highly who are years beyond transition-related interventions. It may be hard to discern where the dissociation is rooted—in gender trauma or other trauma. It is therefore crucial that we treat the dissociation in a manner that respects that multiple interventions—psychological and physical—may be warranted.

The multilayers of these dimensions of gender trauma bear down on our patients, making it intolerable to stay within one's body. It is a unique clinical picture for trans people. Triggers are unavoidable with gender trauma, since our patients need to be in their bodies for us to work through the trauma. This disconnection can lead to some trans people being fairly clumsy (poor proprioception), which is also common in general trauma (Haines, 2015).

The war with the body that many trans people struggle with is illustrated in the higher incidents of non-suicidal self-injury (NSSI) than found in the general population. dickey, Reisner & Juntunen (2015) found trans and gender nonconforming adults had rates of almost 42 percent whereas Grandclerc and colleagues (2016) found a 10 percent incidence in a community sample and 35 percent in a clinical sample of cisgendered adolescents. The most common NSSI were found to be cutting, banging or hitting self, punching, keeping wounds from healing, severe scratching, burning, and pulling hair (dickey *et al.*, 2015). These compulsions are difficult to completely uproot. I believe they are so stubborn because they are formed early in life and many times in response to unwanted puberty and other trauma. It is more easily ameliorated once the patient is living in their affirmed gender, but, in my experience, in times of stress the behaviors will have a brief reappearance. The approach I take is to reorient the act as a signal to the patient that they are vulnerable in some way and need to take action towards self-care and soothing. It is important the patient can take a compassionate stance towards their self since it can feel regressive to engage in these compulsions and judgment can easily swoop in.

This kind of compulsion is particularly connected to interoception since to those with lower IAcc who have difficulty feeling their body and compounding it with shame, the body feels disposable. For others, interoception intersects with self-harm as an effort to relocate the self back into the body. Therefore, the goal is usually a reframing rather than expecting the person to just stop the act. Something needs to replace it to soothe the individual.

Big "T" traumas and the trans body and mind

Not until sexual trauma is worked through will some patients be able to understand their gender. However, for some it will be the opposite: not until they are safely living in their affirmed gender can they approach working through their trauma. I have worked with patients in both situations. It is a delicate process of not pathologizing aversion to sex, while supporting exploration. When working with trans patients who have experienced sexual trauma, it is important to work towards an understanding of what is related to sexual abuse and what is gender trauma when it comes to areas of the body that cannot be touched or sexual acts cannot be performed. These may overlap. Fear-generalization is likely to occur in sexual and gender trauma in my experience. This is due to a lower ability to perceive and identify interoceptive sensations which leads to a generalization of new stimuli into the earlier models (Petersen, von Leupoldt & Van den Bergh, 2015; Robinson & Clore, 2002). Thus, fear-generalization is happening for patients when they begin to experience bodily feelings during sexual contact and they will try to avoid it.

In the beginning, it is better to work towards other avenues of sexual or intimate contact that are accessible. If that is sensate touch on more neutral areas of the body, then that is a place to begin to develop awareness and recognition of positive sensation, eventually moving on to other areas of the body when the patient feels ready. Ready in this instance means it is a stretch but not something that will set off full trauma alarms.

As discussed in the previous chapter, inhibition (the suppression of intrusive thoughts) is a complicating force when it comes to sexual trauma. The individual may already be burning up mental energy by accommodating for bodily incongruence, but when inhibition of sexual trauma is added, it could feel like you're pushing your way through sex, which is less than optimal. A gentle way through this could be meditation. There has been research finding meditation beneficial for cis women who had experienced sexual abuse (Brotto, Basson & Luria, 2008). Mindfulness to the present moment and bodily sensations improved desire, orgasm, sexual satisfaction, distress and general well-being in cis women (Brotto & Heiman, 2007). Meditation training improved their interoceptive awareness, meaning they were quicker to register their physiological responses, thus lowering dissociation. This awareness was correlated with decreases in the barriers to healthy sexual functioning: anxiety, self-judgment, attention.

We know that our thinking decelerates if we are sad, whereas happiness increases our ability to think and focus (Damasio, 2010). We are operating against this force when we are working with someone who is struggling with gender dysphoria, which for many takes the form of depression. This also connects to allostatic load increasing during transition as seen in DuBois and colleagues' (2017) research on trans men. In depression and anxiety there are attentional biases: negative self-view and threat. These set up an anticipation in the individual of aversive body states which translates to body prediction error that activates action (withdrawal or avoidance; Paulus & Stein, 2010). These are the two basic elements involved with gender trauma (as well as general trauma). Before someone understands that their body prediction error is gender dysphoria, they will defensively employ the strategies of withdrawal and avoidance. This is also the case for those who do understand but cannot take action yet to ameliorate it. Paulus and Stein also pose that those who suffer with depression and anxiety have lower signal to noise ratio in relation to their interoceptive signals. This makes it difficult to distinguish between positive and negative afferent signals and which ones are benign signals in one's body (Paulus & Stein, 2010). The relevance for trans patients, who likely have suffered with depression or anxiety (not all trans people suffer with depression or anxiety but the ones who do are more likely to be seen in treatment) is helping them understand their bodily signals. We may also reframe what presents as depression and anxiety as manifestations of gender trauma as a differential diagnosis which will affect treatment approach (hormone treatment may be more appropriate than anti-depressants). When one has felt at war with one's body most of one's life, one can tend to interpret afferent signals as negative or to not register them at all. Compounding this, arousal for those with a trauma history can certainly be experienced by the individual in a range of ways from uncomfortable to frightening.

Barrett and colleagues (2016) proposed that depression is due to variable insensitivity to prediction errors (as well as poor energy regulation and initiative in activity). They refer to it as a locked-in brain. This complicates the clinical picture for someone who needs to be able to register the gendered prediction errors in order to identify the elements of their gender which need intervention. The inefficiency could be set in motion by early traumatic events or circumstances which required a heavy emotional load (Ansell *et al.*, 2012; Barrett *et al.*, 2016; McLaughlin, Sheridan & Lambert, 2014; Sheridan & McLaughlin, 2014). This fatigue can then result in lowering the ability to correct the prediction error (Barrett *et al.*, 2016). Therapeutic intervention should take the form of helping the patient understand and integrate their bodily signals.

Attention to body sensations, particularly to the genital area, should increase sexual arousal (de Jong, 2009). But for some trans people with genital dysphoria and sexual trauma this is problematic, to say the least. By paying attention to other bodily cues like heart rate or breath, one can connect to more neutral body sensations that are still associated with arousal (Greer, 1983). This can be helpful and less fraught for trans folks. Sexually dysfunctional cis men responded better to sensate-focus rather than putting attention on achieving an erection (Heiman and Rowland, 1983). Focusing on sensate touch without the pressure of genital-focused intimacy can lower the expectations and pressure. The person engages in mapping the body with a partner to investigate what areas of the body feel safe to touch and in what manner. If an area feels uncomfortable, they may/should be able to pause and clue into whether the discomfort is due to gender or reminiscent of abuse. The same goes for what feels positive. Does a certain touch or act affirm one's gender? Does feeling aroused feel uncomfortable since arousal triggers memories of the trauma?

There are some for whom the increase in sex drive is traumatizing due to unprocessed sexual trauma that has been repressed or suppressed up to that point. This is hopefully an opportunity in which these traumas can be worked through if the patient is willing. In some cases, the patient is not willing, and may choose to lower their testosterone to suppress their sex drive rather than confront the trauma. There are other experiences where hormone-related changes bring relief regarding trauma. For instance, a trans woman who is comforted to no longer be plagued by erections that only remind her of her abuser. It will likely just postpone having to process the abuse, since trauma will wait for us until we are prepared to confront it. We know productive therapeutic work does not occur until the patient is consciously and unconsciously ready.

The toxic shame of sexual abuse is particularly present when the act or touch that arouses a person is the same action used in the abuse. It may be gender-affirming but that can make it feel all the more complicated. For example, if a trans woman enjoys receptive penetration but that is also an act which occurred during the abuse. Patients can misunderstand this desire as an indication that their gender identity is pathological. Framing sexual interest and desire as healthy as long as it is not bringing harm to the patient, and distinguishing it from repetition compulsion, is a delicate clinical position. A patient may be enacting a repetition in order to master it, for instance by engaging in penetrative sex in the manner it was perpetrated. This may be traumatizing for the patient or it may be the way they are reclaiming that sexual position for themselves and/or affirming their gender through this act. There is not an objective measure for this; it is unique for each individual. Working through the emotional reactions by articulating it in therapy will open up this terrain for investigation.

"Embodiment is the opposite of dissociation" according to Hill-Meyer & Scarborough (2014, p.357). As therapists we are working to anchor our patients back into their bodies, to dislodge the fog of dissociation. We do this by consistently asking them where in their body they are feeling an emotion. The more emotional the language the patient uses in describing their trauma, the better their psychological health (Wardecker *et al.*, 2017). As we know, it is difficult to articulate any trauma, but gender trauma adds a layer of language resistance to this process as demonstrated in Chapter 1. During this work the clinician and the patient need to sustain patience. We must continue to maintain Winnicott's (1991) potential space, to keep that creative space open while holding and containing the frustration and pain.

The other overlap between sexual abuse and gender trauma is that others may have directly or indirectly denied or disconfirmed the trans person's reality. Many a survivor of sex abuse has been told that what they experienced, what just happened, did not happen. A graphic example from the American news is the case of Larry Nassar, who was the doctor for the women's U.S. gymnastics and Michigan State teams. He told the women and girls that the way he sexually abused them was part of the medical treatment. Another example is the child who is told that sexual intercourse is a game played between grandfathers and their grandchildren or outright told that it did not happen. Another example is the child who has the bravery to disclose the abuse, only to be told by their mother that they are lying. These kind of "explanations" of abuse can make the survivor doubt their sense of what they know to be true. There is a similar disconfirmation that happens for TGNC people who are told that what they feel and who they are is not what they know to be true, but what the other says is the truth. One's sense of reality and trust in one's own mind can be undermined.

A short illustration from my practice will discuss some of what I have been describing in this chapter. One patient was thinking about transition when he started treatment with me for depression and anxiety. The mood disorders were manifestations of complex developmental trauma, poor mirroring and poor affect regulation. We have worked together for three years; he is in his mid-thirties. He experienced unwanted sexualized contact from his mother's boyfriend, was subjected to physical violence, witnessed adult sexual activity throughout his childhood, and had a chronic pain condition, NSSI and cancer, along with gender trauma. He has been working through many layers of invasion on and within his body. He was also the only one in his family questioning the inappropriate behavior in his home. The truth was confronted with denial from the adults, disconfirming his reality. In his treatment, he could not explore and work through these traumas until after he began to find more gender equilibrium; otherwise there would not have been a foundation on which to build. There was so much internal and external trauma that it was understandable that he had difficulty with achieving Winnicott's "going-on-being" (1965, p.303). It was not just an insufficient holding environment but one of existential annihilation.

The acts of medical and social transition enabled the foundation, in connection with the therapeutic alliance, to begin to be. As we addressed each of these former traumas, how they were interlaced with gender was delicately understood. For instance, we explored how his bodily trauma may have delayed his recognition of his need to transition. He may have been able to connect to his interoceptive sensations better if he had not needed to dissociate from his body so consistently as a child. Now that he was more present and feeling his body, he realized how anxious he felt most of the time, which increased his self-harm. This awareness was the gateway through which to explore how he could care for his body and emotional life. There was no streamlined trajectory of the treatment. We are working through self-harm, sex, depression, anxiety, relationships, and gender simultaneously. No one is that neatly divided and everyone's therapy is a singular constr-uction. The therapeutic alliance provided mirroring and containment, which are the foundational approaches onto which all subsequent interventions can occur. We are creating the milieu in which he can learn to heal himself.

This chapter's goal was to provide the questions to ask and the proper lens through which to be viewing trauma with TGNC patients. The frame from which the therapist approaches the juncture of gender trauma with other acute and developmental traumas needs to be deliberately humble in order to maintain an open field. Recovery from traumas is possible. The therapist's position of humility has the secondary benefit that when the therapist does make a definitive statement, it is more powerful. Gender is always running in the background of our consciousness, so we should remember that gender trauma is present even in residual forms as well.

Epilogue

My mission has been to illustrate gender as a psycho-physical phenomenon that can be understood through interdisciplinary theories. I have conceptualized gender dysphoria as a free energy, an enhanced interoceptive, proprioceptive and exteroceptive surprise, since the feeling of gender is related to all of our senses and the neuronal processing of them. Developmental considerations and specific clinical issues related to impairment of bodies, sex and trauma have been explored, which I hope will open up further discourse in the clinical and trans studies literature. The etiology of the thread of shame that runs through transphobia from early childhood through the lifespan cannot be forgotten over the course of a treatment. The trajectory of letting go of shame begins with a critical eye on the self and others. One can first soften up this gaze for others. One can slowly lower one's judgment to accepting others (i.e. it is OK for that person to be trans but not for me). This path can move ultimately to self-acceptance: if it is OK for them, maybe it can be OK for me.

I offered the heuristic gender algorithm and how it can be applied towards finding one's gender quotient. The existential question of most trans people is how one accommodates for the body one has been given and created: in private, in public, in sex, in trauma, and in life.

Additionally, the minor and major accumulation of small "t" and big "T" traumas related to shame, stigma and gendered embodiment will hopefully maneuver clinicians in the direction of humble listening and registering of their patients' experiences. Ultimately, the usefulness of the ideas in this book will be determined by those who apply it to themselves. This book reflects the mindset that has helped me to understand and aid others in their becoming fully their own person through psychotherapy. Not everyone needs psychotherapy to accomplish that, but sometimes it is valuable to have someone who can accompany you through that passage.

Psychotherapists and psychoanalysts can be skittish about counselling on physical interventions, but I hope that these chapters have shown that it is not the therapist's job to know anything for the patient, but to be informed enough to accompany the patient to their own knowledge of their self. I hope that I have also demonstrated here that clinical treatment with gender diverse people must include the body in all its perceptional and sensational elements; not just symbolically but tangibly. Perhaps the future will include more collaboration with physical and occupational therapists and creative arts therapists in aiding people to connect to their bodies in order to understand gender and the self. I hope research, particularly on the brain, will come from the framework established here: one in which there is a recognition of gender dissonance as a disruption to core gender and that what form that intervention takes is determined by the individual. We will have very limited knowledge if research stays in the direction of "proving" an etiology as opposed to studying a process in order to help people live more in a "going-on-being" state. One could study whether the processing in a trans person's body matrix is different when using a prosthetic or not during masturbation or sex using brain scans or other technologies. We want to be able to affirm people's experiences in order to direct specific interventional recommendations more broadly to help others.

The clinical orientation and interventions recommended in this book I hope will engage new discourses and developments in the field. I look forward to those conversations and debates. It is always fascinating to learn from colleagues, even if we do not always agree, since it provides an opportunity for us all to stretch. If we could think of gender like water: what appear to be two elements (H_2 and O) form something that can take on many shapes.

The patients involved in this book selflessly offered their experience in order to help others, for which I am deeply grateful. Our talks about the material in this book were immensely generous on their part and profound for me. The privilege of working with these and all my patients has not just provided me with a rich clinical practice but a life well-lived.

References

Ádám, G. (1998) *Visceral Perception: Understanding Internal Cognition.* New York: Plenum Press.

Adams, N., Hitomi, M. & Moody, C. (2017) "Varied reports of adult transgender suicidality: Synthesizing and describing the peer-reviewed and gray literature." *Transgender Health 2*, 1, 60–75.

Aglioti, S., DeSouza, J. & Goodale, M. (1995) "Size-contrast illusions deceive the eye but not the hand." *Current Biology 5*, 6, 679–685.

Ainley, V., Apps, M.A.J., Fotopoulou, A. & Tsakiris, M. (2016) "'Bodily precision': A predictive coding account of individual differences in interoceptive accuracy." *Philosophical Transactions Royal Society B 371*, 1708.

Ainsley, V., Brass, M. & Tsakiris, M. (2014) "Heartfelt imitation: High interoceptive awareness is linked to greater automatic imitation." *Neuropsychologia 60*, 21–28.

Ainsworth, T.A. & Spiegel, J.H. (2010) "Quality of life of individuals with and without facial feminization surgery or gender reassignment surgery." *Quality of Life Research: An International Journal of Quality of Life Aspects of Treatment, Care and Rehabilitation 19*, 1019–1024.

Amodeo, A.L., Vitelli, R., Scandurra, C., Picariello, S. & Valerio, P. (2015) "Adult attachment and transgender identity in the Italian context: Clinical implications and suggestions for further research." *International Journal of Transgenderism 16*, 1, 49–61.

Ansell, E.B., Rando, K., Tuit, K., Guarnaccia, J. & Sinha, R. (2012) "Cumulative adversity and smaller gray matter volume in medial prefrontal, anterior cingulate, and insula regions." *Biological Psychiatry 72*, 57–64.

Apps, M.A.J. & Tsakiris, M. (2014) "The free energy self: A predictive coding account of self-recognition." *Neuroscience Biobehavioral Review 41*, 85–97.

Armel, K.C. & Ramachandran, V.S. (2003) "Projecting sensations to external objects: Evidence from skin conductance response." *Proceedings: Biological Sciences 270*, 1523, 1499–1506.

Auer, M.K., Cecil, A., Roepke, Y., Bulty, C. *et al.* (2016) "12-months metabolic changes among gender dysphoric individuals under cross-sex hormone treatment: A targeted metabolomics study." *Scientific Reports 6*, 1–10.

Badoud, D. & Tsakiris, M. (2017) "From the body's viscera to the body's image: Is there a link between interoception and body image concerns?" *Neuroscience and Biobehavioral Reviews 77*, 237–246.

Baltazar, M., Hazem, N., Vilarem, E., Beaucousin, V., Picq, J.L. & Conty, L. (2014) "Eye contact elicits bodily self-awareness in human adults." *Cognition 133*, 120–127.

Baril, A. (2015) "Transness as debility: Rethinking intersections between trans and disabled embodiments." *Feminist Review 111*, 59–74.

Barlow, D.H. (1986) "Causes of sexual dysfunction: The role of anxiety and cognitive interference." *Journal of Consulting and Clinical Psychology 54*, 140–157.

Barrett, L.F., Quigley, K.S. & Hamilton, P. (2016) "An active inference theory of allostasis and interoception in depression." *Philosophical Transactional Royal Society B 371*: 20160011.

Barrett, L.F. & Simmons, W.K. (2015) "Interoceptive predictions in the brain." *Nature Reviews Neuroscience 16*, 419–429.

Bauer, G.R., Hammond, R., Travers, R., Kaay, M., Hohenadel, K.M. & Boyce, M. (2009) "'I don't think this is theoretical; this is our lives': How erasure impacts health care for transgender people." *Journal of the Association of Nurses in AIDS Care 20*, 5, 348–361.

Beebe, B. & Lachmann, F. (1998) "Co-constructing inner and relational processes: Self and mutual regulation in infant research and adult treatment." *Psychoanalytic Psychology 15*, 1–37.

Berlucchi, G. & Aglioti, S. (2010) "The body in the brain revisited." *Experimental Brain Research 200*, 25–35.

Bigelow, A.E. & Rochat, P. (2006) "Two-month-old infants' sensitivity to social contingency in mother–infant and stranger–infant interaction." *Infancy 9*, 3, 313–325.

Bockting, W.O., Robinson, B.E. & Rosser, B.R.S. (1998) "Transgender HIV prevention: A qualitative needs assessment." *AIDS Care: Psychological and Socio-medical Aspects of AIDS/HIV 10*, 4, 505–525.

Bouvattier, C., Mignot B., Lefèvre, H., Morel, Y. & Bougnères P. (2006) "Impaired sexual activity in male adults with partial androgen insensitivity." *The Journal of Clinical Endocrinology and Metabolism 9*, 9, 3310–3315.

Breslow, A.S., Brewster, M.E., Velez, B.L., Wong, S., Geiger, E. & Soderstrom, B. (2015) "Resilience and collective action: Exploring buffers against minority stress for transgender individuals." *Psychology of Sexual Orientation and Gender Diversity 2*, 3, 253–265.

Broadbent, D.E. (1958) *Perception and Communication.* New York: Pergamon.

Bromberg, P. (1998) *Standing in the Spaces: Essays on Clinical Process, Trauma and Dissociation.* New York: Psychology Press.

Brooks-Gunn, J. & Matthews, W. (1979) *He and She: How Children Develop Their Sex-Role Identity.* Englewood Cliffs, NJ: Prentice Hall.

Brotto, L.A., Basson, R. & Luria, M. (2008) "A mindfulness-based group psychoeducational intervention targeting sexual arousal disorder in women." *The Journal of Sexual Medicine 5*, 1646–1659.

Brotto, L.A. & Heiman, J.R. (2007) "Mindfulness in sex therapy: Applications for women with sexual difficulties following gynecologic cancer." *Sexual and Relationship Therapy 22*, 3–11.

Budge, S.L., Adelson, J.L. & Howard, K.A. (2013) "Anxiety and depression in transgender individuals: The roles of transition status, loss, social support, and coping." *Journal of Consulting and Clinical Psychology 81*, 545–557.

Budhwani, H., Hearld, K.R., Milner, A.N., Charow, R. *et al.* (2018) "Transgender women's experiences with stigma, trauma, and attempted suicide in the Dominican Republic." *Suicide and Life-Threatening Behavior*, January, 1–9.

Burke, S.M., Amir, H., Manzouri, A.H., Dhejne, C., Arver, S., Feusner, J.D. & Savic-Berglund, I. (2017a) "Testosterone effects on the brain in transgender men." *Cerebral Cortex*, 2017, 1–15.

Burke, S.M., Manzouri, A.H. & Savic, I. (2017b) "Structural connections in the brain in relation to gender identity and sexual orientation." *Scientific Reports 7*, 17954.

Burnes, T.R., Dexter, M.M., Richmond, K., Singh, A.A. & Cherrington, A. (2016) "Experiences of transgender survivors of trauma who undergo social and medical transition." *Traumatology 22*, 1, 75–84.

Case, L.K., Brang, D., Landazuri, R., Viswanathan, P. & Ramachandran, V.S. (2017) "Altered white matter and sensory response to bodily sensation in female-to-male transgender individuals." *Archives of Sexual Behavior 46*, 5, 1223–1237.

Cazala, F., Vienney, N. & Stoléru, S. (2015) "The cortical sensory representation of genitalia in women and men: A systematic review." *Socioaffective Neuroscience & Psychology 5*, 26428.

Cerny, J.A. (1978) "Biofeedback and the voluntary control of sexual arousal in women." *Behavior Therapy 9*, 847–855.

Chalmers, D. (2002) "The hidden mind." *Scientific American*, 90–100.

Chrabaszcz, J. & Dougherty, M. (2012) "Deliberations on unconscious thought theory." *Frontiers in Psychology, 3,* 350.

Clark, A. (1999) "An embodied cognitive science." *Trends in Cognitive Sciences 3,* 9, 345–351.

Clark, J.E., Watson, S. & Friston, K.J. (2018) "What is mood? A computational perspective." *Psychological Medicine,* 1–8.

Cohen, S. (1988) "Perceived Stress in a Probability Sample of the United States." S. Spacapan & S. Oskamp (eds) *The Claremont Symposium on Applied Social Psychology. The Social Psychology of Health.* Thousand Oaks, CA: Sage Publications.

Compton, R.J. (2003) "The interface between emotion and attention: A review of evidence from psychology and neuroscience." *Behavioral Cognitive Neuroscience Review 2,* 2, 115–129.

Condry, J. & Condry, S. (1976) "Sex differences: A study of the eye of the beholder." *Child Development 47,* 812–819.

Costantini, M. & Haggard, P. (2007) "The rubber hand illusion: Sensitivity and reference frame for body ownership." *Consciousness & Cognition 16,* 2, 229–240.

Cowie, D., Makin, T.R. & Bremner, A.J. (2013) "Children's responses to the rubber-hand illusion reveal dissociable pathways in body representation." *Psychological Science 24,* 5, 762–769.

Craig, A.D. (2003) "Interoception: The sense of the physiological condition of the body." *Current Opinion in Neurobiology 13,* 500–505.

Craig, A.D. (2009a) "How do you feel – now? The anterior insula and human awareness." *National Review of Neuroscience 10,* 59–70.

Craig, A.D. (2009b) "Emotional moments across time: A possible neural basis for time perception in the anterior insula." *Philosophical Transactions Royal Society B,* 364, 1933–1942.

Craig, A.D. (2011) "Significance of the insula for the evolution of human awareness of feelings from the body." *Annals of N.Y. Academy of Sciences 1225,* 72–82.

Craig, A.D. (2015) *How Do You Feel: An Interoceptive Moment with Your Neurobiological Self.* Princeton, NJ; Princeton University Press.

Crick, F. (1994) The Astonishing Hypothesis: The Scientific Search for the Soul. New York: Simon and Schuster.

Critchley, M. (1979) *The Divine Banquet of the Brain.* New York: Raven Press.

Crucianelli, L., Metcalf, N.K., Fotopoulou, A.K. & Jenkinson, P.M. (2013) "Bodily pleasure matters: Velocity of touch modulates body ownership during the rubber hand illusion." *Frontiers in Psychology 4,* 703.

Damasio (1999) *The Feeling of What Happens: Body and Emotion in the Making of Consciousness*. Wilmington, MA: Mariner Books.

Damasio (2010) Self Comes to Mind: Constructing the Conscious Brain. New York: Random House.

D'Augelli, A.R., Grossmanm A.H. & Starks, M.T. (2006) "Childhood gender atypicality, victimization, and PTSD among lesbian, gay, and bisexual youth." *Journal of Interpersonal Violence 21*, 11, 1–21.

Davis, L.J. (2013) "Introduction: Normality, Power, and Culture." In L.J. Davis (ed.) *The Disabilities Studies Reader*, 4th edition. New York: Taylor and Francis.

de Jong, D.C. (2009) "The role of attention in sexual arousal: Implications for treatment of sexual dysfunction." *The Journal of Sex Research 46*, 2–3, 237–248.

De Preester, H. & Tsakiris, M. (2009) "Body-extension versus body-incorporation: Is there a need for a body-model?" *Phenomenology and the Cognitive Sciences 8*, 3, 307–319.

Devue, C., Collette, F., Balteau, E., Degueldre, C., Luxen, A., Maquet, P. & Brédart, S. (2007) "Here I am: The cortical correlates of visual self-recognition." *Brain Research 1143*, 169–182.

Dickerson, S.S., Gruenewald, T.L. & Kemeny, M.E. (2004) "When the social self is threatened: Shame, physiology, and health." *Journal of Personality 72*, 6, 1191–1216.

dickey, l.m., Reisner, S.L. & Juntunen, C.L. (2015) "Non-suicidal self-injury in a large online sample of transgender adults." *Professional Psychology: Research and Practice 46*, 1, 3–11.

dickey, l.m., Singh, A.A. & Walinsky, D. (2017) "Treatment of Trauma and Nonsuicidal Self-Injury in Transgender Adults." *Pediatric Clinics of North America, 40*, 1, 41–50.

Dijksterhuis, A., Bos, M.W., Nordgren, L.F. & van Baaren, R.B. (2006) "On making the right choice: The deliberation-without-attention effect." *Science 311*, 17, 1005–1007.

Domschke, K., Stevens, S., Pfleiderer, B. & Gerlach, A. (2010) "Interoceptive sensitivity in anxiety and anxiety disorders: An overview and integration of neurobiological findings." *Clinical Psychology Review 30*, 1–11.

DuBois, L.Z. (2012a) "Biocultural Perspectives on Gender, Transitions, Stress, and Immune Function." Accessed on 06/14/18 at http://scholarworks.umass.edu/open_access_dissertations/546.

DuBois L.Z. (2012b) "Associations between transition-specific stress experience, nighttime dip in blood pressure, and C-reactive protein levels among transgendered men." *American Journal of Human Biology 24*, 1, 52–61.

DuBois, L.Z., Everett, B., Puckett, J.A., Juster, R.P. & Sievert, L. (2016) "Body and behavior satisfaction predict depression and anxiety among trans men." Presentation at the World Professional Association for Transgender Health. Amsterdam, Netherlands.

Dubois, L.Z., Powers, S., Everett, B. & Juster, R.P. (2017) "Stigma and diurnal cortisol among transitioning transgender men." *Psychoneuroendocrinology 82*, 59–66.

Dunn, B.D., Galton, H.C., Morgan, R., Evans, D. *et al.* (2010) "Listening to your heart. How interoception shapes emotion experience and intuitive decision making." *Psychological Science 21*, 1835–1844.

Duquette, P. (2017) "Increasing our insular world view: Interoception and psychopathology for psychotherapists." *Frontiers of Neuroscience 11*, 135.

Duschek, S., Werner, N.S., del Paso, G.A.R. & Schandry, R. (2015) "The contributions of interoceptive awareness to cognitive and affective facets of body experience." *Journal of Individual Differences 36*, 110–118.

Edelman, G. (1989) The Remembered Present: A Biological Theory of Consciousness. New York: Basic Books.

Edelman, G. (2004) *Wider Than the Sky: The Phenomenal Gift of Consciousness*. New Haven, CT: Yale University Press.

Edelstein, R.S. (2006) "Attachment and emotional memory: Investigating the source and extent of avoidant memory impairments." *Emotion 6*, 340–345.

Einstein, A. (1961) *Relativity: The Special and General Theory*. New York: Bonanza Books.

Elaut, E., Heylens, G., Van hoorde, B. & De Cuypere, G. (2016) "Sexual functioning and gender-confirming treatment: A European multicenter follow-up study." Findings from ENIGI-Initiative. World Professional Association of Transgender Health Symposium, Amsterdam, Netherlands.

Elbers, J.M.H., Asscheman, H., Seidell, J.C., Megens, J.A.J. & Gooren, L.J.G. (1997) "Long-term testosterone administration increases visceral fat in female to male transsexuals." *The Journal of Clinical Endocrinology and Metabolism 82*, 7, 2044–2047.

Erikson, E. (1963) *Childhood and Society.* New York: Norton.

Ernst J., Boker, H., Hattenschwiler, J., Schupbach, D. *et al.* (2013) "The association of interoceptive awareness and alexithymia with neurotransmitter concentrations in the insula and anterior cingulate." *Social Cognitive and Affective Neuroscience 9*, 857–863.

Esmail, S., Darry, K., Walter, A. & Knupp, H. (2010) "Attitudes and perceptions towards disability and sexuality." *Disability and Rehabilitation 32*, 14, 1148–1155.

Factor, R.J. & Rothblum, E.D. (2007) "A study of transgender adults and their non-transgender siblings on demographic characteristics, social support, and experiences of violence." *Journal of LGBT Health Research 3*, 11–30.

Fairhurst, M.T., Löken, L. & Grossmann, T. (2014) "Physiological and behavioral responses reveal 9-month-old infants' sensitivity to pleasant touch." *Psychological Science 25*, 5, 1124–1131.

Farazandeh, M. (2017) "100 Women: 'Disabled Women Have Sexual Needs Too.'" Accessed on 06/14/18 at www.bbc.com/news/world-42183197.

Farb, N.A., Segal, Z.V. & Anderson, A.K. (2013) "Mindfulness meditation training alters cortical representations of interoceptive attention." *Social Cognitive and Affective Neuroscience 8*, 15–26.

Fernyhough, C. (2012) *Pieces of Light: The New Science of Memory.* London: Profile Books.

Feusner, J.D., Lidström, A., Moody, T.D., Dhejne, C., Bookheimer, S.Y. & Savic, I. (2016) "Intrinsic network connectivity and own body perception in gender dysphoria." *Brain Imaging and Behavior 11*, 4, 964–976.

Fischer, D., Messner, M. & Pollatos, O. (2017) "Improvement of interoceptive processes after an 8-week body scan intervention." *Frontiers of Human Neuroscience 11*, 452.

Fischer, F. (2003) *Reframing Public Policy: Discursive Politics and Deliberative Practices.* Oxford: Oxford University Press.

Fonagy, P. (1997) "Attachment, the Development of the Self, and Its Pathology in Personality Disorders." In C. Maffei, J. Derksen, & H. Groen (eds) *Treatment of Personality Disorders.* New York: Plenum Press.

Fotopoulou, A. & Tsakiris, M. (2017) "Mentalizing homeostasis: The social origins of interoceptive inference." *Neuropsychoanalysis 19*, 1, 3–28.

Fraisse, P. (1984) "Perception and estimation of time." *Annual Review of Psychology 35*, 1–36.

Fraley, R.C., Niedenthal, P.M., Marks, M., Brumbaugh, C. & Vicary, A. (2006) "Adult attachment and the perception of emotional expressions: Probing the hyperactivating strategies underlying anxious attachment." *Journal of Personality 74*, 1163–1190.

Freud, S. (1923) "The Ego and the Id." *The Standard Edition of the Complete Psychological Works of Sigmund Freud, Volume XIX (1923–1925): The Ego and the Id and Other Works.* London: Hogarth.

Freud, S. (1937) "Analysis terminable and interminable." *International Journal of Psycho-Analysis 18*, 373–405.

Friston, K.J. & Stephan, K.E. (2007) "Free-energy and the brain." *Synthese, 159,* 3, 417–458.

Friston, K. (2009) "The free-energy principle: A rough guide to the brain?" *Trends in Cognitive Sciences 13,* 293–301.

Frølund, L. (1997) "Early shame and mirroring." *The Scandinavian Psychoanalytic Review 20,* 1, 35–57.

Fuchs, T. (2003) "The phenomenology of shame, guilt and the body in body dysmorphic disorder and depression." *Journal of Phenomenological Psychology 33,* 2, 223–243.

Furman, D. J., Waugh, C.E., Bhattacharjee, K., Thompson, R.J. & Gotlib, I.H. (2013) "Interoceptive awareness, positive affect, and decision making in major depressive disorder." *Journal of Affective Disorders 151,* 780–785.

Gallagher, S. (2005) *How the Body Shapes the Mind.* Oxford: Oxford University Press.

Gallagher, S. (2011) "Introduction: A Diversity of Selves." In S. Gallagher (ed.) *The Oxford Handbook of the Self.* Oxford: Oxford University Press.

Gallagher, S. & Meltzoff, A. (1996) "The earliest sense of self and others: Merleau-Ponty and recent developmental studies." *Philosophical Psychology 9,* 2, 211–233.

Gallese, V. (2014) "Bodily selves in relation: Embodied simulation as second person perspective on intersubjectivity." *Philosophical Transactions Royal Society B* 369: 20130177.

Gallup, G., Anderson, J. & Platek, S. (2011) "Self-Recognition." In S. Gallagher (ed.) *Oxford Handbook of the Self.* Oxford: Oxford University Press.

Garfinkel, S.N. & Critchley, H.D. (2013) "Interoception, emotion and brain: New insights link internal physiology to social behaviour." *Social Cognitive and Affective Neuroscience 8,* 231–234.

Garfinkel, S.N., Seth, A.K., Barrett, A.B., Suzuki, K. & Critchley, H.D. (2015) "Knowing your own heart: Distinguishing interoceptive accuracy from interoceptive awareness." *Biological Psychology 104,* 65–74.

Geoffard, P.Y. & Luchini, S. (2010) "Changing time and emotions." *Philosophical Transactions Royal Society B 365,* 271–280.

Gergely, G. & Watson, J.S. (1996) "The social biofeedback theory of parental affect-mirroring: The development of emotional self-awareness and self-control in infancy." *The International Journal of Psychoanalysis 77,* 6, 1181–1212.

Gordon, A.R. & Meyer, I.H. (2007) "Gender nonconformity as a target of prejudice, discrimination, and violence against LGB individuals." *Journal of LGBT Health Research 3,* 3, 55–71.

Grady, D. (2015) "Penis transplants being planned to help wounded troops." *The New York Times*, December 6. Accessed on 28/09/18 at https://www.nytimes.com/2015/12/07/health/penis-transplants-being-planned-to-heal-troops-hidden-wounds.html.

Grandclerc, S., De Labrouhe, D., Spodenkiewicz, M., Lachal, J. & Moro, M.R. (2016) "Relations between nonsuicidal self-injury and suicidal behavior in adolescence: A systematic review." *PLoS One 11*, e0153760.

Greer, J.G. (1983) *The Sexual Aggressor: Current Perspectives on Treatment.* New York: Van Nostrand Reinhold.

Grossman, A.H., D'Augelli, A.R., Howell, T.J. & Hubbard, S. (2005) "Parents' reactions to transgender youths' gender non-conforming expression and identity." *Journal of Gay and Lesbian Social Services 18*, 3–16.

Haas, A.P., Rodgers, P.L. & Herman, J.L. (2014) "Suicide attempts among transgender and gender non-conforming adults: Findings of the national transgender discrimination survey." *The Williams Institute*. Accessed on 06/14/18 at https://williamsinstitute.law.ucla.edu/wp-content/uploads/AFSP-Williams-Suicide-Report-Final.pdf.

Hahn, A., Kranzl, G., Küblböck, M., Kaufman, U. *et al.* (2014) "Structural connectivity networks of transgender people." *Cerebral Cortex 25*, 10.

Haines, S. (2015) *Trauma is Really Strange.* London: Jessica Kingsley Publishers.

Hameroff, S. (2018) "Idealism, Panpsychism and Pan-Protopsychism." Plenary. The Science of Consciousness. April 6. Tucson, Arizona.

Hancock, P.A. & Weaver, J.L. (2005) "On time distortion under stress." *Theoretical Issues in Ergonomics Science 6*, 193–211.

Harnishfeger, K.K. (1995) "The Development of Cognitive Inhibition: Theories, Definitions and Research Evidence." In F.N. Dempster & C.J. Brainerd (eds) *New Perspectives on Interference and Inhibition in Cognition.* San Diego, CA: Academic Press.

Heidegger, M. (1962 [1927]) *Being and Time* (trans. J. Macquarrie & E. Robinson). London: Blackwell.

Heiman, J.R. & Rowland, D.L. (1983) "Affective and physiological sexual response patterns: The effects of instructions on sexually functional and dysfunctional men." *Journal of Psychosomatic Research 27*, 2, 105–116.

Henry, D. (2017) *Trans Voices: Becoming Who You Are.* London: Jessica Kingsley Publishers.

Herbert, B.M. & Pollatos, O. (2012) "The body in the mind: On the relationship between interoception and embodiment." *Topics in Cognitive Science 4*, 692–704.

Herman, J.L. (2013) "Gendered restrooms and minority stress: The public regulation of gender and its impact on transgender people's lives." *Journal of Public Management & Social Policy 19*, 65–80.

Hill-Meyer, T. & Scarborough, D. (2014) "Sexuality." In L. Erickson-Shroth (ed.) *Trans Bodies, Trans Selves*. New York: Oxford University Press.

Hill-Soderlund, A.L., Mills-Koonce, W.R., Propper, C., Calkins, S.D. *et al.* (2008) "Parasympathetic and sympathetic responses to the strange situation in infants and mothers from avoidant and securely attached dyads." *Developmental Psychobiology 50*, 4, 361–376.

Hirschfeld, M. (1919/1991) *Transvestites: The Erotic Drive to Cross-Dress*. New York: Prometheum.

Hoekzema, E., Schagen, S., Kreukels, B.P.C., Veltman, D.J. *et al.* (2015) "Regional volumes and spatial volumetric distribution of gray matter in the gender dysphoric brain." *Psychoneuroendocrinology 55*, 59–71.

Hohmann, G.W. (1966) "Some effects of spinal cord lesions on experienced emotional feelings." *Psychophysiology 3*, 2, 143–156.

Honneth, A. (2001) "Invisibility: On the Epistemology of 'Recognition.'" *Aristotelian Society Supplementary Volume 75*, 1, 111–126.

Hua, L.H., Strigo, I.A., Baxter, L.C., Johnson, S.C. & Craig, A.D. (2005) "Anteroposterior somatotopy of innocuous cooling activation focus in human dorsal posterior insular cortex." *American Journal of Physiology Regulatory Integrative and Comparative Physiology 289*, 2, R319–R325.

Hulshoff Pol, H.E., Cohen-Kettenis, P.T., Van Haren, N.E.M., Peper, J. *et al.* (2006) "Changing your sex changes your brain: Influences of testosterone and estrogen on adult human brain structure." *European Journal of Endocrinology 155*, S107–S114.

Ibeñez, A., Gleichgerrcht, E. & Manes, F. (2010) "Clinical effects of insular damage in humans." *Brain Structure and Function 214*, 397–410.

Intersex Society of North America (2006) Clinical Guidelines for the Management of Disorders of Sex Development in Childhood: Consortium on the Management of Disorders of Sex Development. Rohnert Park, CA: ISNA.

Jackson, F. (1982) "Epiphenomenal qualia." *The Philosophical Quarterly 32*, 127, 127–136.

James, W. (1884) "What is an emotion?" *Mind 9*, 188–205.

James, W. (1887) "The Consciousness of Lost Limbs." *Proceedings of the American Society for Psychical Research, 1,* 249–258.

James, W. (1890/1950) *The Principles of Psychology, Volume One.* New York: Dover Publications.

James, S.E., Herman, J.L., Rankin, S., Keisling, M., Mottet, L. & Anafi, M. (2016) "The Report of the 2015 U.S. Transgender Survey." Washington, DC: National Center for Transgender Equality.

Janssen, A., Huang, H. & Duncan, C. (2016) "Gender variance among youth with autism spectrum disorders: A retrospective chart review." *Transgender Health 1,* 1, 63–68.

Janssen, E. & Bancroft, J. (2006) "The Dual-Control Model: The Role of Sexual Inhibition and Excitation in Sexual Arousal and Behavior." In E. Janssen (ed.) *The Psychophysiology of Sex.* Bloomington, IN: Indiana University Press.

Janssen, E. & Everaerd, W. (1993) "Determinants of male sexual arousal." *Annual Review of Sex Research 4,* 211–245.

Janssen, E., Everaerd, W., Spiering, M. & Janssen, J. (2000) "Automatic processes and the appraisal of sexual stimuli: Toward an information processing model of sexual arousal." *The Journal of Sex Research 37,* 2, 8–23.

Joel, D., Berman, Z., Tavor, I.M., Wexler, N. *et al.* (2015) "Sex beyond the genitalia: The human brain mosaic." *Proceedings of the National Academy of Sciences of the United States of America 112,* 50, 15468–15473.

Joffily, M. & Coricelli, G. (2013) "Emotional valence and the free-energy principle." *PLoS Computational Biology 9,* 6, e1003094.

Jordan-Young, R. (2011) *Brain Storm: The Flaws in the Science of Sex Difference.* Cambridge, MA: Harvard University Press.

Kafer, A. (2013) *Feminist, Queer, Crip.* Bloomington, IN: Indiana University Press.

Kandel, E. (2012) *The Age of Insight: The Quest to Understand the Unconscious in Art, Mind, and Brain, from Vienna 1900 to the Present.* New York: Random House Publishing Group.

Kawaguchi, A., Nemoto, K., Nakaaki, S., Kawaguchi, T. *et al.* (2016) "Insular volume reduction in patients with social anxiety disorder." *Frontiers in Psychiatry 7,* 3.

Keo-Meier, C.L., Herman, L.I., Reisner, S.L., Pardo, S.T., Sharp, C. & Babcock, J.C. (2014) "Testosterone treatment and MMPI–2 improvement in transgender men: A prospective controlled study." *Journal of Consulting and Clinical Psychology 83,* 1.

Keo-Meier, C.L. & Fitzgerald, K.M. (2016) "Affirmative Psychological Testing and Neurocognitive Assessment with Transgender Adults." *The Psychiatric Clinics of North America, 40,* 51–64.

Kersting, A., Reuteman, M., Gast, U., Ohrmann, P. *et al.* (2003) "Dissociative disorders and traumatic childhood experiences in transsexuals." *The Journal of Nervous and Mental Disease 191*, 182–189.

Kessler, S.J. & McKenna, W. (1978) *Gender: An Ethnomethodological Approach.* Chicago, IL: University of Chicago Press.

Kleeman, J.A. (1971) "The establishment of core gender identity in normal girls. II. How meanings are conveyed between parent and child in the first 3 years." *Archives of Sexual Behavior 1*, 2, 117–129.

Kohlberg, L. (1966) *A Cognitive-Developmental Analysis of Children's Sex-role Concepts and Attitudes.* Redwood City, CA: Stanford Press.

Koken, J.A., Bimbi, D.S. & Parsons, J.T. (2009) "Experiences of familial acceptance–rejection among transwomen of color." *Journal of Family Psychology 23*, 6, 853–860.

Krahé, C., Paloyelis, Y., Condon, H., Jenkinson, P.M., Williams, S.C.R. & Fotopoulou A. (2015) "Attachment style moderates partner presence effects on pain: A laser evoked potentials study." *Social Cognitive and Affective Neuroscience 10*, 1030–1037.

Kranz, G.S., Wadsak, W., Kaufmann, U., Savli, M. *et al.* (2015) "High-dose testosterone treatment increases serotonin transporter binding in transgender people." *Biological Psychiatry 78*, 8, 525–533.

Lacan, J. (1966) *Ecrits.* New York: W.W. Norton & Company.

Lacan, J. (1977) *The Seminar of Jacques Lacan, Book XI: The Four Fundamental Concepts of Psychoanalysis, 1964.* New York: W.W. Norton & Company.

Laing, R.D. (1962) *The Divided Self.* London: Pelican Penguin.

Langer, S.J. (2014) "Our body project: Mourning and creating the transgender body." *International Journal of Transgenderism 15*, 2, 66–75.

Langer, S.J. (2016) "Trans bodies and the failure of mirrors." *Studies in Gender and Sexuality 17*, 4, 306–316.

Langer, S.J. & Martin, J.I. (2004) "How dresses can make you mentally ill: Examining the gender identity disorder in childhood diagnosis." *Adolescent Social Work Journal 21*, 5.

Lawrence, D.H. (1948) "The acquired distinctiveness of cues." Partially unpublished Yale University dissertation. In N.E. Miller (1992) "Some examples of psychophysiology and the unconscious." *Biofeedback and Self-Regulation 17*, 3, 3–16.

Laws, D.R. & Rubin, H.B. (1969) "Instructional control of an autonomic sexual response." *Journal of Applied Behavior Analysis 2*, 93–99.

Leder, D. (1990) *The Absent Body.* Chicago, IL: University of Chicago Press.

Lewis, M. (1972) "Parents and children: Sex-role development." *School Review 80*, 229–240.

Lewis, M. (1992) *Shame: The Exposed Self.* New York: Free Press.

Lin, C.S., Ku, H.L., Chao, H.T., Tu, P.C. & Li, C.T. (2014) "Neural network of body representation differs between transsexuals and cissexuals." *PLoS ONE 9*, 1, e85914.

Lipson, J. (2017) The MPS Art Therapy Department Fall 2017 Conference: Creative Arts Therapies: Innovation and Integration. Accessed on 06/14/18 at https://vimeo.com/241430827.

Lipson, J. (in press, projected 2019) "Seeking the Uncensored Self: Music Therapy with Transgender Clients." In D. Trottier, K. Long, B. MacWilliams & B. Harris (eds) *Creative Arts Therapies and the LGBTQ Community: Theory and Practice.* London: Jessica Kingsley Publishers.

Lloyd, D.M., Gillis, V., Lewis, E., Farrell, M.J. & Morrison, I. (2013) "Pleasant touch moderates the subjective but not objective aspects of body perception." *Frontiers Behavioral Neuroscience 7*, 207.

Luders, E., Sánchez, F.J., Tosun, D., Shattuck, D.W. *et al.* (2012) "Increased cortical thickness in male-to-female transsexualism." *Journal of Behavioral and Brain Science 2*, 357–362.

Makin, T.R., Holmes, N.P. & Ehrsson, H.H. (2008) "On the other hand: Dummy hands and peripersonal space." *Behavioural Brain Research 191*, 1–10.

Mallorquí-Bagué, N., Bulbena, A., Pailhez, G., Garfinkel, S.N. & Critchley, H.D. (2016) "Mind body interactions in anxiety and somatic symptoms." *Harvard Review of Psychiatry 24*, 53–60.

Manzouri, A., Kosidou, K. & Savic, I. (2015) "Anatomical and functional findings in female-to-male transsexuals: Testing a new hypothesis." *Cerebral Cortex 27*, 2, 1–13.

Martin, C.L. & Ruble, D.N. (2004) "Children's search for gender cues: Cognitive perspectives on gender development." *Current Directions in Psychological Science 13*, 67–70.

Masters, W. & Johnson, V. (1966) *Human Sexual Response.* New York: Bantam.

May, R. (1975) *The Courage to Create.* New York: Norton.

McBee, T.P. (2014) *Man Alive: A True Story of Violence, Forgiveness and Becoming a Man.* San Francisco, CA: City Lights Books.

McLaughlin, K.A., Sheridan, M.A. & Lambert, H.K. (2014) "Childhood adversity and neural development: Deprivation and threat as distinct dimensions of early experience." *Neuroscience Biobehavior Review 47*, 578–591.

Menon, V. & Uddin, L.Q. (2010) "Saliency, switching, attention and control: A network model of insula function." *Brain Structure and Function 214*, 655–667.

Merleau-Ponty, M. (1945/1962) *Phenomenology of Perception.* New York: Routledge.

Mikulincer, M. & Shaver, P.R. (2007) "Boosting attachment security to promote mental health, prosocial values, and inter-group tolerance." *Psychological Inquiry 18*, 3,139–156

Miller, L.C., Murphy, R. & Buss, A.H. (1981) "Consciousness of body: Private and public." *Journal of Personality and Social Psychology 41*, 2, 397–406.

Morgan, R., Marais, C. & Wellbeloved, J.R. (eds) (2010) *Trans: Transgender Life Stories from South Africa.* South Africa: Jacana Media.

Morrison, I., Björnsdotter, M. & Olausson, H. (2011) "Vicarious responses to social touch in posterior insular cortex are tuned to pleasant caressing speeds." *The Journal of Neuroscience 31*, 26, 9554–9562.

Moseley, G.L. & Brugger, P. (2009) "Interdependence of movement and anatomy persists when amputees learn a physiologically impossible movement of their phantom limb." *Proceedings of the National Academy of Sciences USA 106*, 18798–18802.

Moseley, G.L., Gallace, A. & Spence, C. (2011) "Bodily illusions in health and disease: Physiological and clinical perspectives and the concept of a cortical 'body matrix'." *Neuroscience and Biobehavioral Review 36*, 1, 34–46.

Moseley, G.L., Olthof, N., Venema, A., Don, S. *et al.* (2008) "Psychologically induced cooling of a specific body part caused by the illusory ownership of an artificial counterpart." *Proceedings of the National Academy of Sciences of the USA 105*, 35, 13169–13173.

Muller, J. (1985) "Lacan's mirror stage." *Psychoanalytic Inquiry: A Topical Journal for Mental Health Professionals, 5*, 2, 233–252.

Murray, C.D. (2004) "An interpretative phenomenological analysis of the embodiment of artificial limbs." *Disability and Rehabilitation 26*, 16, 963–973.

Niedenthal, P.M., Brauer, M., Robin, L. & Innes-Ker, A.H. (2002) "Adult attachment and the perception of facial expression of emotion." *Journal Personality and Social Psychology 82*, 419–433.

Nikolajsen, L. & Staehelin Jensen, T. (2001) "Phantom limb pain." *British Journal of Anaesthesia 87*, 1, 107–116.

Norman A.S., Farb, N., Segal, Z.V. & Anderson, A.K.(2012) "Mindfulness meditation training alters cortical representations of interoceptive attention." *Social Cognitive and Affective Neuroscience 8*, 1, 15–26.

Nude, R.J., Milliken, G.W., Jenkins, W.M. & Merzenich, M.M. (1996) "Use-dependent alterations of movement representations in primary motor cortex of adult squirrel monkeys." *The Journal of Neuroscience 16*, 2, 785–807.

Oda, H. & Kinoshita, T. (2017) "Efficacy of hormonal and mental treatments with MMPI in FtM individuals: Cross-sectional and longitudinal studies." *BMC Psychiatry 17*, 256.

Oliver, M. (2009) *Understanding Disability: From Theory to Practice.* London: Palgrave MacMillan.

Parkinson, J. (2015) "Gender dysphoria 'cured' by status epilepticus." *Australas Psychiatry 23*, 2, 166–168.

Parshall, M.B., Schwartzstein, R.M., Adams, L., Banzett, R.B. *et al.* (2012) "An official American Thoracic Society statement: Update on the mechanisms, assessment, and management of dyspnea." *American Journal of Respiratory Critical Care Medicine 185*, 436–452.

Paulus, M.P. & Stein, M.B. (2010) "Interception in anxiety and depression." *Brain Structure and Function 214*, 451–463.

Pavlov, I. (1926) *Conditioned Reflexes: An Investigation of The Physiological Activity of the Cerebral Cortex.* Oxford: Oxford University Press.

Perez-Brumer, A., Hatzenbuehler, M.L., Oldenburg, C.E. & Bockting, W. (2015) "Individual- and structural-level risk factors for suicide attempts among transgender adults." *Behavioral Medicine 41*, 3, 164–171.

Petersen S., von Leupoldt, A. & Van den Bergh, O. (2015) "Interoception and the uneasiness of the mind: Affect as perceptual style." *Frontiers of Psychology 6*, 1408.

Pines, M. (1985) "Mirroring and child development." *Psychoanalytic Inquiry: A Topical Journal for Mental Health Professionals 5*, 2, 211–231.

Polanyi, M. (1958) *Personal Knowledge: Towards a Post-Critical Philosophy.* Chicago, IL: Chicago University Press.

Polanyi, M. (1966) *The Tacit Dimension.* Chicago, IL: University of Chicago Press.

Pollatos, O., Herbert, B.M., Mai, S. & Kammer, T. (2016) "Changes in interoceptive processes following brain stimulation." *Philosophical Transactions Royal Society B 371*: 20160016.

Pollatos, O., Jürgen Füstös, T.S. & Critchley, H.D. (2012) "On the generalised embodiment of pain: How interoceptive sensitivity modulates cutaneous pain perception." *Pain 153*, 1680–1686.

Pollatos, O., Kurz, A.L., Albrecht, J., Schreder, T. *et al.* (2008) "Reduced perception of bodily signals in anorexia nervosa." *Eating Behaviors 9*, 381–388.

Pollatos, O., Traut-Mattausch, E. & Schandry, R. (2009) "Differential effects of anxiety and depression on interoceptive accuracy." *Depression and Anxiety 26*, 167–173.

Porges, S.W. (2003) "Social engagement and attachment: A phylogenetic perspective." *Annals of the New York Academy of Sciences 1008*, 31–47.

Pyne, J. (2017) "Arresting Ashley X: Trans youth, puberty blockers and the question of whether time is on your side." *Somatechnics 7*, 1, 95–123.

Quattrocki, E. & Friston, K. (2014) "Autism, oxytocin and interoception." *Neuroscience Biobehavioral Review 47*, 410–430.

Rachlin, K. (2018) "Medical transition without social transition: Expanding options for the privately-gendered body." *Trans Studies Quarterly 5*, 2.

Radden, J. (2011) "Multiple Selves." In S. Gallagher (ed.) *Oxford Handbook of the Self.* Oxford: Oxford University Press.

Ramachandran, V.S. (2004) *A Brief Tour of Human Consciousness.* New York: Pi Press.

Ramachandran, V.S. & Blakeslee, S. (1998) *Phantoms in the Brain.* New York: Quill/Harper Collins.

Ramachandran, V.S. & McGeoch, P.D. (2008) "Phantom penises in transsexuals: Evidence of an innate gender-specific body image in the brain." *Journal of Consciousness Studies 15*, 1, 5–16.

Ramstead, M.J.D., Badcock, P.B. & Friston, K.J. (2018) "Answering Schrödinger's question: A free-energy formulation." *Physics of Life Reviews 24*, 1–16.

Rand, E. (2014) "Hips." *Transgender Studies Quarterly 1*, 1–2, 98–99.

Recanzone, G.H., Merzenich, M.M., Jenkins, W.M., Grajski, K.A. & Dinse, H.R. (1992) "Reorganization of the hand representation in cortical area 3b of owl monkeys trained in a frequency-discrimination task." *Journal of Neurophysiology 67*, 5.

Reyes, M.S., Alcantara, A.E., Reyes, A.C., Yulo, P.L. & Santos, C.P. (2016) "Exploring the link between internalized stigma and self-concept clarity among Filipino transgenders." *North American Journal of Psychology 18*, 2, 335–344.

Robbins-Cherry, S. (2016) "Sexual discovery after surgery." Presentation as part of plenary panel for Trans+Sexualities Conference, Psychotherapy Center for Gender and Sexuality: a Division of the Institute for Contemporary Psychotherapy, November 5, New York.

Robinson, M.D. & Clore, G.L. (2002) "Belief and feeling: Evidence for an accessibility model of emotional self-report." *Psychological Bulletin 128*, 934–360.

Robles, R., Fresán, A., Vega-Ramírez, H., Cruz-Islas *et al.* (2016) "Removing transgender identity from the classification of mental disorders: A Mexican field study for ICD-11." *Lancet Psychiatry 3*, 850–859.

Rochat, P. (2009) *Others in Mind: Social Origins of Self-Consciousness.* New York: Cambridge University Press.

Rochat, P. & Morgan, R. (1995) "Spatial determinants in the perception of self-produced leg movements by 3- to 5-month-old infants." *Developmental Psychology 31*, 626–636.

Rodriguez, O. (2008) The Baseball Project Video. Accessed on 06/15/18 at https://vimeo.com/32670719.

Rognoni, E., Galati, D., Costa, T. & Crini, M. (2008) "Relationship between adult attachment patterns, emotional experience and EEG frontal asymmetry." *Personality and Individual Differences 44*, 909–920.

Rood, B.A., Reisner, S.L., Puckett, J.A., Surace, F.I., Berman, A.K. & Pantalone, D.W. (2017) "Internalized transphobia: Exploring perceptions of social messages in transgender and gender-nonconforming adults." *International Journal of Transgenderism 18*, 4, 411–426.

Rothbart, M.K., Ziaie, H. & O'Boyle, C.G. (1992) "Self-regulation and emotion in infancy." *New Directions for Child and Adolescent Development 5*, 7–23.

Saketopoulou, A. (2014) "Coming undone: Developmental perspectives on massive gender trauma." *Journal of the American Psychoanalytic Association 62*, 5, 773–806.

Sambo C.F., Howard, M., Kopelman, M., Williams, S. & Fotopoulou, A. (2010) "Knowing you care: Effects of perceived empathy and attachment style on pain perception." *Pain 151*, 687–693.

Sartre, J.P. (1992) *Being and Nothingness: A Phenomenological Essay on Ontology.* New York: Washington Square Press.

Schaefer, M., Flor, H., Heinze, H.J. & Rotte, M. (2007) "Morphing the body: Illusory feeling of an elongated arm affects somatosensory homunculus." *Neuroimage 36*, 700–705.

Scharff, D.E. (1982) *The Sexual Relationship.* London: Routledge & Kegan Paul.

Schulz, A. & Vögele, C. (2015) "Interoception and stress." *Frontiers in Psychology 6*, 993.

Scott, J. (1988) *Gender and the Politics of History.* New York: Columbia University Press.

Searles, J.R. (1997) *The Mystery of Consciousness.* New York: The New York Review of Books.

Seavey, C., Katz, P. & Rosenberg Zalk, S. (1975) "Baby X: The effect of gender labels on adult responses to infants." *Sex Roles 1*, 2, 103–109.

Serano, J. (2007) *Whipping Girl: A Transsexual Woman on Sexism and the Scapegoating of Femininity.* California: Seal Press.

Seth, A.K. (2009) "Explanatory correlates of consciousness: Theoretical and computational challenges." *Cognitive Computation 1,* 50–63.

Seth, A.K. (2013) "Interoceptive inference, emotion, and the embodied self." *Trends Cognitive Science 17,* 565–573.

Seth A.K. & Friston, K.J. (2016) "Active interoceptive inference and the emotional brain." *Philosophical Transactions Royal Society B 371,* 1708.

Seth, A.K., Suzuki, K. & Critchley, H.D. (2012) "An interoceptive predictive coding model of conscious presence." *Frontiers in Psychology 2,* 395.

Shai, D. & Belsky, J. (2011) "When words just won't do: Introducing parental embodied mentalizing. *Child Development Perspectives 5,*3, 173–180.

Shakespeare, T. (1992) "A Response to Liz Crow." *Coalition,* September, 40–42.

Shapiro, F. (2001) *Eye Movement Desensitization and Reprocessing: Basic Principles, Protocols and Procedures.* New York; Guilford Press.

Shelley, C.A. (2008) *Transpeople: Repudiation, Trauma, Healing.* Toronto: University of Toronto Press.

Sheridan, M.A. & McLaughlin, K.A. (2014) "Dimensions of early experience and neural development: Deprivation and threat." *Trends Cognitive Science 18,* 580–585.

Sherman, R.A. & Sherman, C.J. (1983) "Prevalence and characteristics of chronic phantom limb pain among American veterans. Results of a trial survey." *American Journal of Physical Medicine 62,* 227–238.

Shipherd, J.C., Maguen, S., Skidmore, W.C. & Abramovitz, S.M. (2011) "Potentially traumatic events in a transgender sample: Frequency and associated symptoms." *Traumatology 17,* 2, 56–67.

Shoemaker, S. (2011) "On What We Are." In S. Gallagher (ed.) *The Oxford Handbook of the Self.* Oxford: Oxford University Press.

Siebers, T. (2012) "A Sexual Culture for Disabled People." In R. McRuer & A. Mollow (eds) *Sex and Disability.* Durham, NC: Duke University Press.

Simmons, W.K., Avery, J.A., Barcalow, J.C., Bodurka, J., Drevets, W.C. & Bellgowan, P. (2013) "Keeping the body in mind: Insula functional organization and functional connectivity integrate interoceptive, exteroceptive, and emotional awareness." *Human Brain Mapping 34,* 2944–2958.

Sinzig, J., Dagmar, M., Bruning, N., Schmidt, M. & Lehmkuhl, G. (2008) "Inhibition, flexibility, working memory and planning in autism spectrum disorders with and without comorbid ADHD-symptoms." *Child and Adolescent Psychiatry and Mental Health 2*, 4.

Spade, D. (2003) "Resisting medicine, re/modeling gender." *Berkeley's Women's Law Journal 18*, 1, 15–37.

Sterling, P. (2014) "Homeostasis vs allostasis: Implications for brain function and mental disorders." *Clinical Review and Education: Neuroscience and Psychiatry 71*, 10.

Sterling, P. & Eyer, J. (1988) "Allostasis: A new paradigm to explain arousal pathology." In S. Fisher & J. Reason (eds) *Handbook of Life Stress, Cognition and Health*. Hoboken, NJ: John Wiley & Sons.

Stiegler, B. (1998) *Technics and Time, 1. The Fault of Epimetheus*. Stanford, CA: Stanford University Press.

Straayer, C. (2016) Inaugural International Trans Studies Conference, University of Arizona, Tucson.

Strigo, I.A. & Craig, A.D. (2016) "Interoception, homeostatic emotions and sympathovagal balance." *Philosophical Transactions Royal Society B 371*, 1–9.

Swaab, D. & Bao, A. (2013) "Sexual Differentiation of the Human Brain in Relation to Gender-Identity, Sexual Orientation, and Neuropsychiatric Disorders." In D.W. Pfaff (ed.) *Neuroscience in the 21st Century*. New York: Springer.

Tepper, M.S. (2000) "Sexuality and disability: The missing discourse of pleasure." *Sex and Disability 18*, 283–290.

Testa, R.J., Habarth, J., Peta, J., Balsam, K. & Bockting, W. (2015) "Development of the gender minority stress and resilience measure." *Psychology of Sexual Orientation and Gender Diversity 2*, 1, 65–77.

Thompson, S. (1975) "Gender labels and early sex role development." *Child Development 46*, 339–347.

Tillich, P. (1952) *The Courage to Be*. New Haven, CT: Yale University Press.

Tremain, S. (2006) "On the Government of Disability: Foucault, Power, and the Subject of Impairment." In L.J. Davis (ed.) *The Disability Studies Reader*. New York: Routledge.

Trevarthen, C. (1979) "Communication and Cooperation in Early Infancy: A Description of Primary Intersubjectivity." In M.M. Bullowa (ed.) *Before Speech: The Beginning of Interpersonal Communication*. New York: Cambridge University Press.

Tsakiris, M. (2010) "My body in the brain: A neurocognitive model of body ownership." *Neuropsychologia 48*, 703–712.

Tsakiris, M. & Haggard, P. (2005) "The rubber hand illusion revisited: Visuotactile integration and self attribution." *Journal of Experimental Psychology: Human Perception and Performance 31*, 80–91.

Uddin, L.Q. (2014) "Salience processing and insular cortical function and dysfunction." *Nature Reviews Neuroscience 16*, 1, 55–61.

UPIAS (Union of the Physically Impaired Against Segregation) and the Disability Alliance (1976) *Fundamental Principles of Disability* booklet. Accessed on 07/02/18 at https://disability-studies.leeds.ac.uk/wp-content/uploads/sites/40/library/UPIAS-fundamental-principles.pdf.

Uvnäs-Moberg, K., Handlin, L. & Petersson, M. (2014) "Self-soothing behaviors with particular reference to oxytocin release induced by non-noxious sensory stimulation." *Frontiers in Psychology 5*, 1529.

Van de Grift, T.C., Kreukels, B.P., Elfering, L., Özer, M. *et al.* (2016) "Body image of transmen: Multidimensional measurement of the effects of mastectomy." *The Journal of Sexual Medicine 13*, 11, 1778–1786.

Van der Kolk, B. (2015) *The Body Keeps the Score: Brain, Mind, and Body in the Healing of Trauma.* New York: Penguin Books.

VanderLaan, D.P., Santarossa, A., Nabbijohn, A.N., Wood, H., Owen-Anderson, A. & Zucker, K. (2017) "Separation anxiety among birth-assigned male children in a specialty gender identity service." *European Child & Adolescent Psychiatry 27*, 1, 89–98.

Van Seters, A. & Slob, A. (1988) "Mutually gratifying heterosexual relationship with micropenis of husband." *Journal of Sex and Marital Therapy 14*, 98–107.

van Stralen, H.E., van Zandvoort, M.J., Hoppenbrouwers, S.S., Vissers, L.M., Kappelle, L.J. & Dijkerman, H.C. (2014) "Affective touch modulates the rubber hand illusion." *Cognition 131*, 1, 147–158.

Verschuren, J.E., Geertzen, J.H., Enzlin, P., Dijkstra, P.U. & Dekker, R. (2015) "People with lower limb amputation and their sexual functioning and sexual wellbeing." *Disability and Rehabilitation 37*, 3, 187–193.

Vitelli, R. & Riccardi, E. (2010) "Gender identity disorder and attachment theory: The influence of the patient's Internal Working Models on psychotherapeutic engagement and objective. A study undertaken using the Adult Attachment Interview." *International Journal of Transgenderism 12*, 241–253.

Vygotsky, L.S. (1981) "The Genesis of Higher Mental Functions." In J.V. Wertsch & M.E. Sharp (eds) *The Concepts of Activity in Soviet Psychology.* New York: Routledge.

Wardecker, B.M., Edelstein, R.S., Quas, J.A., Cordón, I.M. & Goodman, G.S. (2017) "Emotion language in trauma narratives is associated with better psychological adjustment among survivors of childhood sexual abuse." *Journal of Language and Social Psychology 36*, 6, 1–26.

Weeks, S.R. & Tsao, J.W. (2010) "Incorporation of another person's limb into body image relieves phantom limb pain: A case study." *Neurocase 16*, 6, 461–465.

Weinstein, S. & Sersen, E.A. (1961) "Phantoms in cases of congenital absence of limbs." *Neurology*, Oct, 11, 905–911.

Weisz, J., Balázs, L. & Ádám, G. (1988) "The effect of monocular viewing on heartbeat perception." *Psychophysiology 31*, 370–374.

Wiegel, M., Scepkowski, L. & Barlow, D. (2007) "Cognitive-affective processes in sexual arousal and sexual dysfunction." In E. Janssen (ed.) *The psychophysiology of sex.* Bloomington, IN: Indiana University Press.

Wiens, S. (2005) "Interoception in emotional experience." *Current Opinion in Neurology 18*, 442–447.

Wierckx, K., Elaut, E., Van Hoorde, B., Heylens, G. *et al.* (2014) "Sexual desire in trans persons: Associations with sex reassignment treatment." *International Society for Sexual Medicine 11*, 107–118.

Wierckx, K., Van Caenegem, E., Elaut, E., Dedecker, D. *et al.* (2011) "Quality of life and sexual health after sex reassignment surgery in transsexual men." *International Society for Sexual Medicine 8*, 3379–3388.

Wilkerson, A. (2012) "Normate Sex and Its Discontents." In R. McRuer & A. Mollow (eds) *Sex and Disability.* Durham, NC: Duke University Press.

Winnicott, D.W. (1958) "The capacity to be alone." *The Journal of Psychoanalysis 39*, 416–420.

Winnicott, D.W. (1965) "Ego distortion in terms of true and false self in maturational processes and the facilitating environment." In M. Masud & R. Khan (eds) *The Maturational Processes and the Facilitating Environment: Studies in the Theory of Emotional Development.* London: Hogarth Press and the Institute of Psycho-Analysis.

Winnicott, D.W. (1971) *Playing and Reality.* New York: Routledge.

Wittmann, M. (2009) "The inner experience of time." *Philosophical Transactions Royal Society B 364*, 1955–1967.

World Health Organization (2014) "Eliminating forced, coercive and otherwise involuntary Sterilization: An interagency statement." OHCHR, UN Women, UNAIDS, UNDP, UNFPA, UNICEF and WHO. Accessed on 06/15/18 at www.who.int/reproductivehealth/publications/gender_rights/eliminating-forced-sterilization/en.

WPATH (World Professional Association for Transgender Health) (2011) *Standards of Care, Version 7.* Accessed on 07/02/18 at www.wpath.org.

Young, I.M. (2011) *Justice and the Politics of Difference.* New Jersey: Princeton University Press.

Zahavi, D. (2014) "Self & Other: Exploring Subjectivity, Empathy and Shame." In S. Gallagher (ed.) *The Oxford Handbook on the Self.* New York: Oxford University Press.

Zautra, A., Fasman, R., Davis, M. & Craig, A.D. (2010) "The effects of slow breathing on affective responses to pain stimuli: An experimental study." *Pain 149*, 12–18.

Zubiaurre-Elorza, L., Junque, C., Gómez-Gil, E. & Guillamon, A. (2014) "Effects of cross-sex hormone treatment on cortical thickness in transsexual individuals." *The Journal of Sex Medicine 11*, 1248–1261.

Zubiaurre-Elorza, L., Junque, C., Gómez-Gil, E., Segovia, S. *et al.* (2013) "Cortical thickness in untreated transsexuals." *Cerebral Cortex 23*, 2855–2862.

Zucker, K., Nabbijohn, A.N., Santarossa, A., Wood, H. *et al.* (2017) "Intense/obsessional interests in children with gender dysphoria: A cross-validation study using the Teacher's Report Form." *Child Adolescent Psychiatry Mental Health 11*, 51, 1–8.

About the Author

S.J. Langer is a writer and psychotherapist in New York City, U.S.A. where he maintains a private practice. He is on faculty at the School of Visual Arts in both the MPS Art Therapy and Humanities & Sciences departments. He holds a Masters in Social Work from New York University and a Bachelor of Fine Arts in Filmmaking from the School of Visual Arts. His most recent academic article "Trans bodies and the failure of mirrors" was the co-winner of the Symonds Prize from Studies in Gender and Sexuality.

Index